2004 POET

ONCE UPON A RHYME

IMAGINATION FOR
A NEW GENERATION

Norfolk
Edited by Donna Samworth

 Young**Writers**

First published in Great Britain in 2004 by:
Young Writers
Remus House
Coltsfoot Drive
Peterborough
PE2 9JX
Telephone: 01733 890066
Website: www.youngwriters.co.uk

SB ISBN 184460 434 9

Foreword

Young Writers was established in 1991 and has been passionately devoted to the promotion of reading and writing in children and young adults ever since. The quest continues today. Young Writers remains as committed to engendering the fostering of burgeoning poetic and literary talent as ever.

This year's Young Writers competition has proven as vibrant and dynamic as ever and we are delighted to present a showcase of the best poetry from across the UK. Each poem has been carefully selected from a wealth of *Once Upon A Rhyme* entries before ultimately being published in this, our twelfth primary school poetry series.

Once again, we have been supremely impressed by the overall high quality of the entries we have received. The imagination, energy and creativity which has gone into each young writer's entry made choosing the best poems a challenging and often difficult but ultimately hugely rewarding task - the general high standard of the work submitted amply vindicating this opportunity to bring their poetry to a larger appreciative audience.

We sincerely hope you are pleased with our final selection and that you will enjoy *Once Upon A Rhyme Norfolk* for many years to come.

Contents

Ben Vozza (9)	16
Joe Hatton (9)	16
Algar Epps (10)	17
Olivia Pearce (9)	17
Perry George (9)	18
Chloe Hodge (10)	18
Ben Handley (9)	19
Natasha Aspin (10)	19
Joshua Brewer (9)	20
Amy Partridge (9)	20

Middleton VC Primary School

James Everitt (11)	21
Lauren Depear (11)	21
Shannen Wiles Van Dyke (10)	22
Stacey Softley (11)	22
Oliver Mitchell (10)	22
Elizabeth Morgan (9)	23
Thomas Harrod (10)	23
Scott Burns (11)	24
Reece Stannard (11)	24
Alex Gore (11)	25
Simone Fox (10)	25
Laura Plain (9)	25
Matthew Bacon (9)	26
Alex Peart (10)	26
Ashley Manning (10)	27
Neil Fuller (10)	27
Ryan Murray (11)	28
Elliot John (9)	28
Shane Allard (10)	28
Vicky Plain (9)	29
Jess Taylor (11)	29
Bethany Deadman (10)	30
Bethany Murray (9)	30

Queensway Junior School

Polly Robertson (10)	31

St Andrew's CE VA Primary School, North Lopham

James Baillie (9)	31
Sorrel Lawrence (9)	32
Grant Carter (10)	32
Sam Goddard (11)	33
Holly Walker (10)	33
Craig Thompson	34
Lily Smith (9)	34
Thomas Fitzpatrick (11)	35

St Martha's RC Primary School, Kings Lynn

Guy France (9)	35
Joseph Thomas Parish (9)	35
Shaun Mckenna (9)	36
Saffron Rudd (9)	36
Damien Watt (8)	36
Dylan James Yates (11)	37
Kirsty Miller (7)	37
Ewan France (8)	38
Sebastian Ashwell	39
Katie Reed (10)	39
Karl Johnson (7)	40
Maria Hodkinson (7)	40
Niamh McGovern (7)	40
Joseph Doherty (7)	41
Matthew Cody (7)	41
Jack Tucker (8)	42
Rebecca Harrington (8)	42
Hannah Gore (7)	43
Martyn Nantongwe (7)	43
Ben Waite (10)	44
Nicolle Miller (10)	44
Ciaran Hodkinson (10)	45
Abigail Auker (9)	45
Samantha Caunt (9)	45
Martin Gibbs (9)	46
Vincent Hart (9)	46
Joel Matthews (9)	47
William Robinson (9)	47
Eleanor Smith (10)	47
Maria L'Estrange (10)	48

Lauren Rasberry (11)   48
Daniel Cody (11)   49
Ashley Sheen (11)   49
Carolyn Dales (11)   50
Carla Dye (10)   50
Samantha Harrington (11)   51
Colleen Nolan (10)   51
Jessamine Hopkins (10)   52
Holly Ambrose (10)   52
Rebecca Leventhall (10)   53
Megan Nolan (8)   53
Melrie Antoinette A Fabian (8)   54
Bairavi Bala (9)   54
Séan McQuaid (8)   54
Guy Williams (9)   55
Steven Frazer (9)   55
Kerrie Gilboy (9)   55
Josephine E Partridge (8)   56
Molly Hill (9)   56
Katie Smith (8)   57
James France (10)   57
Sam Pressling (9)   57
Emma Tilbrook (9)   58
Jack Reed (8)   58
Ella Bliss (8)   58
Victoria Wiglusz (7)   59
Courtney Beales (8)   59
Siobhan Kavanagh (7)   60
Alexander Havercroft (8)   60

St Michael's VA Middle School, Bowthorpe
Marcus Ashley (11)   61
Casey Quadling (10)   61
Jake Armes (10)   62
Georgia Heggie (11)   62
Farah Nizal (9)   63
Kelly Crome (8)   64
Jasmine Crotch (10)   64
Callum Smith (8)   65
Jake Cranston (9)   65
Luke Goodswen (8)   66

John Chapman (11)	66
Nikita Bilham (9)	67
Alice Dover (11)	67
Joshua Moore (8)	68
Iain Savage (10)	68
Craig Turner (10)	69
Josh Bugg (9)	69
Jade Hudson (10)	70
Lauren Bunn (9)	70
Will Chapman (8)	71
James Frost (8)	71
Bethany Howard (10)	71
Thomas Davies (8)	72
Sophie Bush (8)	72
Charley Barker (8)	73
Antonio Wedral (8)	73
Matthew Manning (9)	74
Jacob Pearson (9)	74
Ashleigh Felstead White (9)	74
Shannon Vince (9)	75
Robert George (9)	75
Ryan Jones (8)	76
Christopher Kinnier (9)	76

St Nicholas House School, North Walsham

Eleanor Brighton (7)	76
Joe Annison (8)	77
Alexander Whitbread (10)	77
Joe Oakey (10)	78
Madeline Buxton (9)	78
Annabel Crane (8)	78
Elliott Palmer (10)	79
Luke Robson (9)	79
Charlotte Bacon (9)	80
Henry Harrison (10)	81
Henry Hale (9)	81
Miles Hodges (8)	81
Alice Harvey (9)	82
Henry Dewing (10)	82
John Neville (11)	83
Emily Gair (10)	83

Hazel Cheung (11)   84
Ben Brighton (10)   84

Saxlingham Primary School
Adam Nelson (10)   85
Lucie Santander (10)   85
Kingsley J White (10)   85
Alfie Chapman (11)   86
James Chadwick (10)   86
Holly Flegg (10)   87
James Burrough (8)   87
Gregory Edwards (9)   88
Caitlin Stone (8)   88
Daniel Burlingham (9)   89
Claudia May St Quintin (8)   89
John Reeve (8)   89
Zachary Nelson (8)   90
Charlie Chadwick (8)   90
Jarrod Stone (9)   90

Shelton With Hardwick Community School
Mark Goddard (10)   91
Jake Atherall (10)   92
Chloe Loftus (8)   93
Joseph Sieveking (10)   94
Madeline Tyler (8)   95
Jessica Hoskins (10)   96
Ellen Goddard (8)   96
Natalie Sieveking (8)   97

Weasenham VC Primary School
Stefany Barham (10)   97
Duncan Butler (9)   98
James Cruise (9)   98
Harriett Spall (10)   99
Ben Dawes (10)   99
Imogen Matthews (10)   100
Naomi Beardsley Best (9)   100
Ira Everett   101
Millie Baker Lynch (7)   101

Stewart Junior Bell (10)   102
Kyle Watts (10)   102
Sophie Newton (9)   103
Georgia Large (9)   103
Jake Rimmer (8)   104

Woodland View Middle School

Scott Dack (11)   104
Georgia Livock (10)   105
Francesca Cullum (9)   106
Emma Goodson (8)   106
Hannah Fox (8)   107
Liam Smith (8)   107
Jaydene Guyton (8)   108
Abigail Clements (8)   108
Hannah Airdrie (8)   109
Peter Broughton (11)   109
Kieran Long (8)   110
Georgie Locke (9)   110
Tom Johnson (8)   111
Ricki Guyton (8)   112
Jack James (8)   112
Jessica Wright-Carruthers (9)   112
Charlie Warren (8)   113
Josie Burnham (8)   113
Iain Dix (9)   114
Elizabeth Fiddy (9)   114
Jack Mollicone (9)   115
Harry Partner (9)   115
Savannah Foster (9)   116
Liam Ogle (9)   116
Bethany Wade (10)   117
Luke Plumstead (9)   117
Connor Elliott (9)   117
Charlotte Curson (9)   118
Shaun Earl (9)   118
Charlotte Stephens (10)   119
Poppy Segger (8)   119
Adam Cooper (9)   120
Matthew Rolls (9)   120
Georgina Fiddy (9)   121

The Poems

Baby Rhino

Baby rhino is a slate-grey mass
which plods about the savannah
enjoying the cool, cool sludge
under the trees.

He is as blind as a bat
but hears everything you do.
He's always as alert
as
there could be a predator
around any corner,
So baby rhino plods towards
the quiet waterhole.
Suddenly from behind a tree
comes a lion much taller than he.
Roar!

Charles Watts (10)
Carleton Rode VAP School

There Was A Young Snake

There was a young snake from Leeds
Who couldn't stop eating leaves
He tried a pie
Thought he would die
So he went back to eating leaves.

Ellen Kennedy (10)
Carleton Rode VAP School

My Cat Pippin

My cat Pippin is a big fat thing,
She is a British short hair and a tabby too.
Just a bit older than me.
We thought she was a boy,
but turned out to be a girl!
'Spit, spit, spit!'
She's spotted a bird.
'Spit, spit, spit!'
She's spotted a dog.
'Spit, spit, spit!'
She's spotted a horse.
Is the whole world coming to
admire my cat Pippin?
My cat Pippin is as cunning
as a wolf.
Her eyes are just like street lamps,
Pippin is a fat cat who sleeps for
almost half the day
Spending the other half either eating,
drinking or spying on the outside world.
Oh, she's my only puddy-cat.

Kirsten Chicot (11)
Carleton Rode VAP School

My Cat Saphie

My cat Saphie is the best there could ever be,
He's grey and fluffy and begs for food.
He's cute and loyal and oh so fussy,
On a wet day he goes out fluffy
And comes in curly.
Saphie's eyes are like shiny marbles,
He has several habits like
Coming in with wet paws or
Scratching at the bedroom doors.
He goes crazy, sometimes he chases
His brother Thomas up and down the stairs.
He sometimes jumps up on chairs and
Tries to steal the dinner.
We do hope he'll get thinner.
We got him when he was four weeks old,
Because he had lost his mother,
He was as skinny as a rat and as little
As a gerbil.
He also has several nicknames
Like Raffysat or Saphierat.
Oh he's a lovely pussy cat.

Katy Thompson (10)
Carleton Rode VAP School

The Stalking Polar Bear

The polar bear starts its long stalk,
As silent as a grave,
It walks gracefully like a lion
Swinging its head for a scent.
The polar bear steps onto an ice float
Spotting a diving seal.
He dives into the perishing cold water after it,
The seal escapes from danger
By swimming a little faster.
Angrily the polar bear swims around
Then leaves the water,
Giving out a loud bellow, like a buffalo in pain.
The polar bear starts to scavenge
Looking all around.
He camouflages himself in the snow
With his creamy white fur,
He goes to sleep, desperate for food.

Hanna Green (10)
Carleton Rode VAP School

Seasons

Spring is a time of joy
For a girl and boy.
Summer is a season with a flaming sun
When everybody has fun.
Autumn with leaves drifting down,
While others fly around.
Finally there's winter with a huge, bare sky,
While the white clouds say goodbye,
The sun shines, glittering bright,
As the silver crescent appears at night.

Dalia Chowdhury (11)
Colman Middle School

Hurricane

Forceful winds, mighty cruel
What is it?
It hacks up roads, crippling people.
What is it?
Wind gets angry, fearful people start to cry
What is it?
Taking everything in its way, destroying villages
What is it?
Cars are gone, people going crazy
What is it?
Dying down but not stopped
What is it?
It's devastating -
It must have been the hurricane!

Kieran Lambert (11)
Colman Middle School

Rap Non-Stop

Well, Friday night has come around,
me and the guys are gonna
head down town,
we're gonna forget all the
troubles we've got,
and dance our way into the
night, non-stop.
The crowd shouts, 'Hey
you're 'A' okay!'
Your moves, your grooves
the way you sway,
but now it's time to end this rap,
don't you worry 'cause we'll
be back!

Daniel Annison (11)
Colman Middle School

Beach

Soft sleek sand twirling around the sky,
Colourful boats sailing in front of me.
Playful dolphins splashing in the sea,
Then a brightly coloured frisbee travels
Across my head.
Queues of people wanting lots of ice cream.
Then all of a sudden the beach is clear.

Megan Haselton (11)
Colman Middle School

Elves

Small, gentle things, dancing on the ground
But others cannot see them when they look around
Wearing dainty outfits
Running up a tree
Elves are very friendly and
Only seen by me!

Oliver Stone (11)
Colman Middle School

The Wee Men

The wee men fought wee dragons
The wee dragons fled
The wee men cheered, 'Hooray! Hooray!'
They drank, two to a pint
They all ran when they saw a spider
Heroes aren't always the bravest!

Benjamin Meade (11)
Colman Middle School

Silly Rhyme

Playing in the sun having so much fun,
When I went home I fed my dog a bone.
My mum was there and she'd lost all her hair.
I asked my mum, 'Are you ill?'
'Go away darling, I'm watching The Bill.'
I went to the shops and I saw so many crops,
I tried to pick some but I got caught
By the cops.
I went back home, all the way on my own.
I got some food but I wasn't in the mood.
It was munchy, munchy, then it went
Crunchy, crunchy!

Nazia Sheik (11)
Colman Middle School

My Sister

My baby sister cries each night
The tears I see shines through the light.
When she gets thirsty, she calls for a drink
She tries to say thank you, but cannot speak.
Her soft gentle hair floats around
Like an angel, away from the ground.
Her tiny toes and tiny hands
Are soft and silky, as if they were sand.
She crawls like a spider onto my lap
As I entertain, she goes, clap clap!
When the day ends she says, 'Night, night!'
I tuck her in her blankets and say,
'Sleep tight!'

Soohyun Sun (10)
Colman Middle School

Fairies

Fairies, so sweet and gentle,
Their skin the colour of pearls.
Their eyes gleaming, passion filled,
From the top of the Sierras.

They always swing above the clouds,
With candy dust that falls,
Sprinkling joyful souls,
Whilst dancing round with elves.

Their wings are such a flutter,
When the spotlights come down,
And pixies dance about
For night has come around.

Kelly Nappin (11)
Colman Middle School

The Dolphin

There are very many of these intelligent creatures
And they all have countless features.
Their skin so smooth
Their mouth so wide.
They glide through the sea
They must have so much pride.
But I haven't seen them -
Maybe you have?
They've got a beautiful body, so sleek and toned
I love them, don't you?
They're called dolphins.

Clare Woods (10)
Colman Middle School

Things Everywhere

Things in the corner
Things in the sky
Things upon the table
And no one knows why
Round things, square things
Furry and blue
There's so many now,
I don't know what to do!

Dexter Herd (11)
Colman Middle School

Land Of Fun

The land is good
No parents!
How does that sound to you?
You can play all the time and
Have some fun
And don't worry about school.

Jonathan Wade (10)
Colman Middle School

The Dolphin

Body streamlined and blue,
There's nothing the dolphin can't do.
He splashes in the ocean
His tail pushing him beneath the water.
His body gliding through the glistening sea,
Moving like a shadow,
Jumping with ease.

Jennifer Whitmore (10)
Colman Middle School

Football

Noise grows louder as the crowd start to cheer
Ball skidding across the green grass
The goal is near
Number 5 makes a pass
The goalie saves
Then it's out for a corner.

The ball's booted into all players in sight
But then the whistle goes, they've started a fight
Now it's on the penalty spot
It's in the back of the net
All players pleased and very, very hot.

Gabby Cason (10)
Colman Middle School

A Puppy

A puppy as soft as a feather
A puppy gleaming gold
Playing in the garden
Getting freezing cold

A puppy so cute
A puppy going crazy
Feeling really active
But later feeling lazy

A puppy sound asleep
We can't hear a peep.

Molly Ashley (10)
Colman Middle School

The Creature

There's a creature under my bed
I know that!
He growls at night.
I hear him and he goes mumble, rumble,
grumble, crunch!
Sometimes I see his green glowing eyes,
I hear bubbling and screeching.
I find goo spilling out,
It's a creature under my bed.

Reuben Thompson (11)
Colman Middle School

Pets

I once had a cat called Kim
Who got thrown out into the bin
I once had a parrot called Jake
Who was slashed by a rake
I once had a dog called Andy
Who died after eating too much candy
I once had a mouse called Lord
Who was stabbed by a sword
I still have a rat called Clive
Who thankfully is still alive.

Elliott Revell (10)
Colman Middle School

Summer

Sun shining
Birds singing
Fun on the beach eating picnics
Water flowing down the streams
Warm camping holidays, having
Lovely dreams.

Louis Atkins (10)
Colman Middle School

Charlie's First Steps

Cheeky Charlie climbs on my bed
And snuggles up for comfort
Cheeky Charlie crunching crisps
'Mmmm!' he says, 'Yum!'
Cheeky Charlie loves his bath
He splashes all my friends
Cheeky Charlie steps toward me -
I can't believe my eyes.

Chantelle Pinder (11)
Colman Middle School

Winter

Winter is wonderful,
Everyone's garden is as white as can be,
All day long we sledge down hills.
As snowmen's shadows dance across the landscape
The ice-cold sun floats across the sky.
Frozen lakes
People's hats on tight.
The white sky sends chills around my body
As that first snowflake lands on my rosy cheek.
The delicate feeling, the tingling cold,
That's why I love the winter.

Alexandra Wiggins (11)
Colman Middle School

Fantasy

Stars twinkling, moon shining
Something moving in the night,
Fairies talking and sparkling
So beautiful like the stars above.

Gary Cory (10)
Colman Middle School

Fairy Ring

Dainty wings, tiny smile,
Can you guess what I can see?
Frilly frocks and floaty hair,
Dancing in the midnight air,
Golden dust that glistens bright,
In the lovely springtime light
Dancing happily in a ring,
When the fairies start to sing.

Saskia Jayne Vinnels (11)
Colman Middle School

Dawn

Sun rises, birds awake and start to sing
Dogs bark and flowers dance in the soft wind
The sky turns blue and the sun
Glows gold, the clouds float and the
Bees fly, squirrels scurry from tree to tree
Along the morning dew, children play
And babies wail, trees are still and
Leaves are falling.
All is calm in a beautiful morning.

Laura Roffey (10)
Colman Middle School

The Moon

The moon woke up on the tired
side of the bed,
Rain beating down on the ground
and it lit up the village, roofs and houses.
The wind is like a giant fan blowing
the clouds away.
The rain stops, the ground looks silver
as the moon's light, lights up the countryside.

Sebastian Harvey (9)
Little Plumstead VA Primary School

Norwich Cathedral

Norwich Cathedral is a peaceful place
Where people come and pray
There are spectacular stone pillars
That reach the ceiling in the cathedral.

The vaulted ceiling is as high as the sky,
Incredible bosses are carved into the ceiling,
They all tell wonderful Bible stories.

There are magical brightly coloured stained glass windows
That glisten in the sunlight.
The cathedral has stood for hundreds
And hundreds of years.

The organ is another spectacular thing,
It can play low and high.
Six thousand pipes are in the organ and
It can play many different tunes.
Sounds of the organ fill the air.
Ghostly shadows and strange sounds
Haunt the cathedral.

Nancy Partridge (9)
Little Plumstead VA Primary School

The Moon

I just woke up from another day's sleep,
Now I glow like a giant marble in the sky.
The clouds race over me like grey stallions,
Suddenly they cover me completely,
So I'm plunged into darkness,
Then they disappear
So I'm allowed to glisten on the river
And make it look like a long silver snake.

Eloise Ayers (9)
Little Plumstead VA Primary School

The Cathedral

When you step one foot into the cathedral
it's like Heaven has struck,
the window behind you sparkles
like stars in the sky.

The pillows swirl right up to the top
it's like an everlasting slide.
The organ roars like a fierce gorilla.

The great bosses are carved into the roof
the wonderful Thomas Gooding was buried
in the wall to be noticed and to go
to Heaven with God.

Take a look for yourself!

Brooke Randall (9)
Little Plumstead VA Primary School

The Ancient Cathedral

The marvellous standing cathedral of Norwich has seen
a threatening past.
The cathedral has seen its last.
The bosses there, they lie, telling the story of their life in time.
The bodies of saints - there they lie,
Their souls looking up to the sky.
There stands Thomas Gooding, there he cries.
He waits for God's Judgement Day, in time.
There the history lies right inside his very eyes.
Nine hundred years of Norwich Cathedral have passed
And we pray to God, long may it last.

Robert Anderson (10)
Little Plumstead VA Primary School

The Cathedral

As I entered the building it towered over me,
It was as clean as God's heart.
The spectacular smell was like an enchantment
From Heaven.

Monks' cloaks, as dark as the dark ages,
But their spirit, as bright as the sun.
They live behind the magnificent cathedral,
They work in the cloisters of this superb cathedral.

The organ sounds like thunder
And whispers like a flute.
The window explodes with colour
And the sun blasts through the blinding windows.

Ben Vozza (9)
Little Plumstead VA Primary School

The Cathedral

The door opens as the day begins,
I have seen the monks and
The Civil War,
I have seen the peasants
Walk the floor.

I am made for God, the people
Who founded me, their hearts
Were full of joy.
I remember the days when the
Bosses were carved into me.
Those hardworking people, carving
All day and night in that small
And tight space.
Now I close my doors as the
Darkness wraps me up in another night.

Joe Hatton (9)
Little Plumstead VA Primary School

Untitled

The moon emerged on the evil side of bed.
He destroyed the shield of blue happiness to reveal darkness.
The only light was from a UFO with alien brilliance.
The graveyard
Lurked black but the mist was still visible to near viewers.
The moon was bored
So it made a flood by raising the sea level.

It was nearing 6am
The battle between the sun and the moon was about to begin.
The other fighters - the planets joined in the fight as well.
That caused a full planet line-up,
In the end, the sun won so it was day once again.

Algar Epps (10)
Little Plumstead VA Primary School

Untitled

The rain rushed hard, pattering on the floor.
Soon came the lightning,
It looked like a silver slithering snake.
I couldn't sleep as the sounds kept me awake.

The wind shook my room
It howled and trembled,
I screamed and ran across my bedroom.
Then there was hail as well as wind and rain.
Then it went, as quickly as it came.

Olivia Pearce (9)
Little Plumstead VA Primary School

The T-Rex

Once I was proud
Once I was king of the dinosaurs
Once I went hunting
Now I'm extinct.

Once I could roar
Once I could fight
Once I was massive
Now I'm extinct.

Once I had sharp teeth
Once I could breathe
Once I ate meat
Now I'm extinct!

Perry George (9)
Little Plumstead VA Primary School

The Storm

The sky is a blue atmosphere
It makes the clouds appear,
The blossom shatters.
Then!
All happiness is destroyed to ashes,
Now I'm frightened and the clouds race over me
Like grey stallions.
Now I am plunged into fate,
I have no choice but to joust the storm
And when peace comes, all will glow
Like a giant marble in the sky.

Chloe Hodge (10)
Little Plumstead VA Primary School

Trees

Once I was fifteen feet high,
Once I had lots of leaves
Once I was wide,
Now I'm firewood.

Once I was in a forest,
Once there were nests in me.
Once I was proud
Now I'm burning.

Once I was tall,
Once I had roots.
Once I had bark on me,
Now I'm burnt to a crisp.

Ben Handley (9)
Little Plumstead VA Primary School

The Cathedral

As I walk to the entrance, the doors open like a flock of wings
The stained glass window is very eye-catching, like a beam of light.
Echoes rule the room with racing shadows.
The spectacular black tombs appear as if they were blinding water.

It makes me feel like an ant,
The roof has roof bosses.
It's like a coat of Christianity, making the place superb
As if it's the palace of silence.

It's not bloodshot-red, it's a smooth cream coat with peace.

Natasha Aspin (10)
Little Plumstead VA Primary School

Holiday

Once I was on holiday
Once I was happy
Once I was free
Now I'm back at school

Once I was fed up
Once I was bored
Once I was swimming
Now I'm back at school

Once I was a boat
Once I was happy
Once I was walking
Now I'm back at school.

Joshua Brewer (9)
Little Plumstead VA Primary School

The Moon

Tonight the moon went down to the dark, damp cellar
and glistened through the thin glass windows.
Outside he looked at the mist and on the grass
he saw the wet silvery dew.
He went back outside and shone on the flowers
and made their petals glow.
The moon could glow forever but
he couldn't always be seen.

Amy Partridge (9)
Little Plumstead VA Primary School

A Morning Spent By The River Nar

Water like ice, freezing our legs,
The soft, sandy bed seeping through our toes;
The tiny trout glide along
When under their breath the tiny bubbles as light as if humming a song
A kingfisher, like a blue bolt of lightning
Darting back and forth
When the green woodpecker is catching food for its young
All together that's what I like about the outdoor life.

James Everitt (11)
Middleton VC Primary School

Sun

The sun burning
Is a fireball
Shining and staring
Flying in the sky.

The sweating hot sun
Is a red-hot tennis ball
Rushing up across the sky
Going anywhere and everywhere.

The blazing hot sun
Is a red-hot oven
Smiling, but tired
Sleeping tight
Good night.

Lauren Depear (11)
Middleton VC Primary School

A Modern Version Of T S Eliot's Prelude

The winter evening settles down
With sound of TV in the street.
Six o'clock
Simpson's tune sings to the beat
Dirty chips at your feet
And now I'm being called for tea.
The rain falls pattering on the car
A herd of boys kick a ball
And someone is making a phone call.

Shannen Wiles Van Dyke (10)
Middleton VC Primary School

An Up To Date Version Of 'Prelude' By T S Eliot

The winter evening settles down
With the sounds of TV in the street.
Six o'clock
Mum calls me in for tea.
Every minute she's thinking of me.
At the corner of the street
A lonely taxi sits and waits,
Beeping its horn
Its lights beaming on everyone who walks past.

Stacey Softley (11)
Middleton VC Primary School

Limerick From Lynn

There was an old man from King's Lynn
He lived in a smelly dustbin
He ate raw fish
Off a small dish
And went on a diet to become thin.

Oliver Mitchell (10)
Middleton VC Primary School

Fire Poem

The fire racing through the dry undergrowth
Is a leopard with burning yellow and black fur,
Prowling and roaring,
Crackling with every tread.

The fire prancing through the dead trees
Is a roe deer with a fiery coat,
Leaping and charging,
Burning the bushes.

The fire slithering through every gap in the forest,
Is a scaly snake wrapping itself around a flaky branch,
Flickering and spitting,
Hissing as it touches water.

Elizabeth Morgan (9)
Middleton VC Primary School

Fire

The fire jumping
Is a ghost
Screaming and shouting
Roaring on the roof.

The fire smoking in my house
Is a speeding sports car
Crackling and sparkling
Sizzling.

The fire breathing
Is a panther pouncing
Steaming and bursting
Flaming.

Thomas Harrod (10)
Middleton VC Primary School

Fire Personification Poem

The fire warming my house
Is a herd of children giving off heat
Charging and running
Singing so loud.

The fire, smelling, burning my house
Is an African elephant
Stomping and howling
Swishing its tail.

The fire gushing with colour
Is a parrot
Squawking and speaking
Singing with pride.

Scott Burns (11)
Middleton VC Primary School

Snow Poem

The snow, white as a polar bear,
Sounds like he's hunting on the house,
Quietly
Trip, trop; he's looking for a fish.

The snow chilling me like an icy cave
For the snow beast.

The snow like a blizzard
Blowing and throwing snowballs.

Reece Stannard (11)
Middleton VC Primary School

Hunger

Hunger is like a little mouse
Nibbling away at your tummy
As if it was cheese.

Hunger is as if someone is beating you up from inside
Not stopping until
You give it food.

Alex Gore (11)
Middleton VC Primary School

'Prelude' By Simone

The winter evening settles down
With The Simpson's tune filling the street,
The light trickling of the rain
Pitter-pattering on the concrete,
Mum calling me in for tea
I run with glee then
Flickering of lights in the bedrooms
As people settle down to sleep.

Simone Fox (10)
Middleton VC Primary School

Sun Poem

The sun shimmering gently on the roof
Is a cheetah
Running and skipping
Brightening up the sky

The sun glimmering around my house
Is a mouse
Squeaking and eating
Running from the cat.

Laura Plain (9)
Middleton VC Primary School

A Morning By The River Nar

The water was twinkling,
The trees were rustling,
The birds were singing,
And we were working.

The swans and cygnets were sleeping,
The leaves were spinning,
The grass was swaying,
And we were playing.

The trout were swimming,
And the kingfisher was flying.
We were leaving,
And everything was singing.

Off we went, walking,
And everyone was talking.

Matthew Bacon (9)
Middleton VC Primary School

The Fire

The fire burning in my house
Is like a herd of leopards
Running through the desert.

The crackling is like a scorpion
Running through the hot steaming desert

The fire beaming into my eyes
It's still crackling away,
Is like a torch in my eyes.

Alex Peart (10)
Middleton VC Primary School

The Rain

The rain thumping on the roof
Is like an angry rhino,
Stomping and stamping,
Being naughty.

The woodwork is rotten from the rain,
Like a caterpillar has been munching
Hungry and stuffing
His little stomach.

The rain is knocking like a woodpecker digging
Looking and searching
For his prey.

Ashley Manning (10)
Middleton VC Primary School

House Fire

The fire prowling around my house
Is a fierce dog
Licking the tips of treetops
Burning and singeing.

The fire stalking around my house
Is a disease
Spreading around my house
Daring to go further.

The fire biting away at my house
Is a snake
Gradually burning the prey
Rearing, ready to strike.

Neil Fuller (10)
Middleton VC Primary School

The Simpsons' Poem

(Based on 'Prelude' by T S Eliot)

The winter evening settles down
With TV's glow shining on the street.
Six o'clock,
Channel changes to Homer putting up his feet.
Comes on Bart Simpson
We see Chief Wiggun
At the corner of the street.
I see Millhouse, the Itchy and Scratchy cat house
And mouse.

Ryan Murray (11)
Middleton VC Primary School

Time

The time ticking
Is a hamster
Crawling and taking
Chunks out of its food.

The time slowing
Is an ice cube
Melting and turning
Into water over a burning fire.

Elliot John (9)
Middleton VC Primary School

Limerick

There was an old Viking from Lynn
Who thought he would try out the gym.
But when he got there
He had nothing to wear
So he went back and sat in the bin.

Shane Allard (10)
Middleton VC Primary School

Thunder

The thunder bangs and crashes
Like a roaring lion,
Snoring loudly.
The thunder roars through corridors
Blowing doors and swooping in the hall.

The thunder screams loudly and fiercely
Like a shark
Bashing against the waves.

Vicky Plain (9)
Middleton VC Primary School

Time Passing

The time is ticking
Like a cheetah
Moving so fast
This minute will soon be past.

The time is ticking
Like a cuckoo,
Calling each hour
On top of the tower.

Every hour chiming
Is a magical beast,
Ticking and tocking
There will be no stopping.

Jess Taylor (11)
Middleton VC Primary School

The Disease

The *disease* spreading round
Is a monstrous snake,
Killing and running,
Throwing people's lives away.

The *disease* prowling round my school
Is a crocodile on water,
Rumbling and growling.

The *disease* stalking round my friends
Is a lion in a tree,
Roaring and purring.

Bethany Deadman (10)
Middleton VC Primary School

The Sun

The sun shining in the house
Is as bright as a lion's mane
Prowling and crawling
Brightening up the sky

The sky shimmering in the window
Is a cheetah's skin
Crawling and sneaking
Roaring through the sunlight.

Bethany Murray (9)
Middleton VC Primary School

Just Take A Seat . . .

Just take a seat . . . I insist,
We may talk and share ideas with each other.
Just take a seat . . . I insist
Even if it's with your baby brother.

Just take a seat . . . I insist,
You may do your homework tonight,
Or sit down to dinner, most polite.

Just take a seat . . . I want you to
The world could be a better place,
With words from me to you.

Polly Robertson (10)
Queensway Junior School

Possum

(This poem is dedicated to my ancient cat)

Slowly slinking,
A great, grey ripple,
Sliding along,
Yet suddenly, hesitant, jerky, tense . . .

A splash of colour,
A silver streak,
A ripping, roaring,
Waterfall of fur,
Claws, teeth, blood . . .
And silence.

Slowly slinking,
A grey ripple
That feels old and wise, yet
Young and daring
Spoken, and yet unspoken . . .
'Hello, can I come in now?'

James Baillie (9)
St Andrew's CE VA Primary School, North Lopham

The Old Oak Tree

The old oak tree
Sat in the garden
Its swing creaking as it
Swung from side to side,
The children grown up
Gone!

Then with a jump,
A child bounced over
And sat on the swaying swing.

'I have a friend,'
He said to the tree.
And the tree dropped a flower
On the child's hair.

And the swing rocked
From side to side.

Sorrel Lawrence (9)
St Andrew's CE VA Primary School, North Lopham

My Dog

Like a spring ready to
Explode
Chasing his tail
Bounding around with bone
A black shadow
Frozen in the garden
Then
Night falls
He drops dead by the fire
Ear still raised
My dog.

Grant Carter (10)
St Andrew's CE VA Primary School, North Lopham

City

Smell of petrol wafting through the air
Hum of the engine
Beep of the horn
Swish of the wipers

Empty shops with huge black eyes
Toy shops full of light and wonder

Ringing mobiles
Clipping of ladies' shoes
Clattering of boxes
Chatty children

Chatty
    Chattering
        Clipping
            Ringing
                Swish
                    Beep
                        Hum
                            Smell.

Sam Goddard (11)
St Andrew's CE VA Primary School, North Lopham

Sea Horse

Horses canter onto the pebbly beach,
Spray flying into the bay,
I watch them prance, I watch them leap,
I always stop and see and stay.

Holly Walker (10)
St Andrew's CE VA Primary School, North Lopham

Fishing

Fishing is so calm and gentle,

Like a calm and warm sea,
A gentle splashing at your feet,
Relaxing to some until!
A twitching and another,
A cranking of the reel,
Then a screaming of the reel,
A fish now,
Pull the rod up high,
As high as the trees,
Fighting the power of carp or barbel
Then, after a long exhausting fight,
The fisherman wins
His grand prize - a mere
Photo of him and his beautiful fish.

Craig Thompson
St Andrew's CE VA Primary School, North Lopham

The Sea

I am the sea,
I can tell you that.
Not to be boastful but
I have lots of friends.
I roar across the great open space,
The moon shines above me,
And lights up the place.
I don't mind ships sailing across me,
Because I am the sea,
And I am great.

Lily Smith (9)
St Andrew's CE VA Primary School, North Lopham

Grandma's Dog

A serious-looking Airedale,
But loopy is he,
Black and brown splodges,
Still full with glee!
Follows his nose, not his brain!
Barmy, maybe dumb,
Ready to pounce on anything which may come,
An energetic playful soul,
Totally nuts but a whole lot of fun!

Thomas Fitzpatrick (11)
St Andrew's CE VA Primary School, North Lopham

Smoking

Smoking is bad for your health.
It causes lung cancer.
Why do people smoke?
'For fun,' some people say.
'But why?' the smokers say,
'What's wrong with it?'

Guy France (9)
St Martha's RC Primary School, Kings Lynn

Crime!

There once was a man called Ronald Reagan.
A man called Michael Jackson robbed him.
Ronald sent the FBI to catch him.
They saw other men try and match him
But they just couldn't find Michael Jackson!

Joseph Thomas Parish (9)
St Martha's RC Primary School, Kings Lynn

Bond

Bond is cool,
Bond is great,
He is the best hero of them all,
He runs as fast as a bullet
Out of a speeding gun,
Oh! If only I could be
Bond's only son!

Shaun Mckenna (9)
St Martha's RC Primary School, Kings Lynn

School Dinners

My belly rumbling, what could it be?
I've had my breakfast,
It's not time for tea.

Dring, Dring, yes, it's finally here,
My belly's starting to cheer,
Curry, chips, pizza, I think.

Now the problem is,
I can't find a seat!

Saffron Rudd   (9)
St Martha's RC Primary School, Kings Lynn

What Is Green?

Grass is green, like leaves
coming from the ground.

Caterpillars climb up stalks,
I like carpets that are green.

I love eating broccoli,
green means go.

I like cold mint ice cream
and lovely round peas.

Damien Watt (8)
St Martha's RC Primary School, Kings Lynn

Snakes

A snake slithers,
A snake squirms,
They hiss and hiss until they find food,
They squeeze every breath out of an animal's body,
They attack,
They spit to kill,
Some rattle,
Some roll,
Some bite,
Some eat each other,
Some don't,
But overall
I prefer corn snakes.

Dylan James Yates (11)
St Martha's RC Primary School, Kings Lynn

White

White is a wedding,
Snowy days,
Frosty white and puffy clouds,
Ice cream for dessert.
Up in the sky,
The moon shining bright
Giving us its light,
A tiny bit of snow falling
On my hand.
I love white snowmen.
A rubber is white.
White is the best.
I love white.
It's my favourite colour.

Kirsty Miller (7)
St Martha's RC Primary School, Kings Lynn

Blue

Blue is a sense,
just painted with blue paint.
A clean St Martha's
sweat shirt too.
Blue is a gel pen
ready to colour.
A crayon as well.
Blue can be waves
running through
water and
blue is jeans
and jumpers too.
Navy-blue joggers
are just the same too.
Blue will be an
electric guitar
dying to play.
Blue can be
Jack's rubber too.
Blue are eyes
looking at you.
Blue is sorrowful.
Blue is always a
thin felt tip,
a puddle like a
reflection.
And a cloth
with blue
and a colour shining blue.
It's paints, crayons
and all those things,
and a pen writing words.
A folder, a holder
or something blue,

a reading book cover
with blue.
And an
enormous whale.
And how would you live without it?

Ewan France (8)
St Martha's RC Primary School, Kings Lynn

Sick

Teacher says, 'Hello.'
Pupil says, 'Goodbye.'
Teacher says, 'Why?'
Pupil says, 'I'm ill.'
Teacher says, 'No, you are not!'
Pupil says, 'Bleurghh!'
He just threw up on the teacher.
The teacher says, 'Goodbye!'

Sebastian Ashwell
St Martha's RC Primary School, Kings Lynn

Farm Trouble

It's a pity to come from the city
I don't know how to work on a farm!
I find farming quite charming,
But cow poo alarming.
Today on the farm a sheep bit my arm,
So I think I'll go back to the city!

Katie Reed (10)
St Martha's RC Primary School, Kings Lynn

What Is Yellow?

The burning sand,
the gleaming sun,
the sunflower and daisies grow.
Slippery butter,
shiny stars at night,
and yellow makes you feel bright
like a spicy curry.

Karl Johnson (7)
St Martha's RC Primary School, Kings Lynn

Smell

The smell of roast dinner is like a fighting sword,
The smooth waves in the sea are calm as can be,
The smell of fish is slippery as a jellyfish,
The smell of petrol is smooth,
The smell of lemons is bitter,
Brandy is tasty on Christmas pudding,
The smell of orange juice is as fresh as can be,
The drainpipe is smelly as can be,
The smell of roses is lovely as can be.

Maria Hodkinson (7)
St Martha's RC Primary School, Kings Lynn

I Feel

I feel snowflakes falling on my nose,
cold snow cuts my hands.
Ice cream slips down my front,
and petrol smells as it burns my hands.
Lotioned hands burn in the sun.

Niamh McGovern (7)
St Martha's RC Primary School, Kings Lynn

Smells

I smell the food that's on my plate
And the drinks that I drink.
I love the smell of petrol
And the smell of juicy lemons.
No one likes the ocean.
I wash my hair with shower gel,
Perfume my mum sprinkles.
The flowers I smell from the window sill
And brand new shoes I wear.
I smell the biscuits my mum cooks,
I love the engine's smell.
The smelly drains I smell,
Mum smells like the ironing
And fresh air
I smell every day.

Joseph Doherty (7)
St Martha's RC Primary School, Kings Lynn

Smells

The smell of the rain
running down the drain.
Roast potatoes roasting
in the oven.
The fresh air whistling
through the foggy mist.
I love the smell of petrol,
the smell of flowers in the field,
the smell of perfume that my mum wears,
I love the smell of new shoes.

Matthew Cody (7)
St Martha's RC Primary School, Kings Lynn

Sounds

Sounds are people splashing in the sea
pitter-patter goes the rain
swish, swish goes the sea
whoosh goes the wind.
People chatting.
Boom goes the balloon
scratch, scratch goes your cat
bark, bark the dog goes
crunching goes like this
crunch, crunch, crunch
squeak, squeak the pigeon goes.

Jack Tucker (8)
St Martha's RC Primary School, Kings Lynn

What Is Green?

Green is the colour
of grass and bushes.
Green is the colour
of grapes that are tasty!
Your face goes green when you're feeling sick
so you need a bottle of green juice drink!
Green is the colour
of people's jumpers
plucking them with holes as they go by.
Gel pens, felt tips,
they all make a mess, on your test.

Rebecca Harrington (8)
St Martha's RC Primary School, Kings Lynn

White

White is very cold frost,
The clouds above,
The snow below.
I like the white board,
It's fun to play on.
I like the white polar bears
Who live in the frost and snow.
Trousers and T-shirts,
They can all be white.
Ropes, cardboard, paint, rubbers, blinds and clothes,
They can all be white.
White is the colour of these things.

Hannah Gore (7)
St Martha's RC Primary School, Kings Lynn

Red

Red is a love that you give
to someone who you love.

Red is the lovely sunset
that is in the sky.

Red is the lipstick
that you put on your lips
when you are going somewhere special.

Red are red roses that
prickle if you touch them.

Red is a colour that is
bright in the dark night.

Martyn Nantongwe (7)
St Martha's RC Primary School, Kings Lynn

Sunday Roast

Sunday roast
making toast,

Carrots cooking
potatoes burning,

Dad's rushing
Mum's brushing,

Gravy's smelling yummy
all ready for my tummy,

It's all ready, yum, yum
time for all the fun,
eating, chewing, gulping
and having lots of fun.

Ben Waite (10)
St Martha's RC Primary School, Kings Lynn

My School Is Great

School is wicked, there's places to go and things to do,
School is fun, you do lots of things,
It's a holy and calming place,
You'll have lots of thoughts.
You get sad times and good times,
You can share them with people too,
School is a place for everyone,
Everyone is loving, caring.
Everyone is welcome in a special place like this,
School is great, you get lots of friends and teachers that care.

Nicolle Miller (10)
St Martha's RC Primary School, Kings Lynn

Friends

F riends are kind. So you should be the same.
R espect all your friends the same.
I always have to play with my friends.
E njoy all your friend's happiness.
N ever hurt your friends or you will lose them.
D on't ignore your friends too much.
S hare with all your friends.

Ciaran Hodkinson (10)
St Martha's RC Primary School, Kings Lynn

The Lion

The lion has a golden mane
and under that a clever brain
and in that brain he has a thought
a thought of eating that meal he caught.

Abigail Auker (9)
St Martha's RC Primary School, Kings Lynn

Air Hostess Romance

'Air hostess I like the way you dress.
I'll see you soon in the hotel room for a holiday romance'.
Your eyes glisten, you really listen when you look at me.
Stay with me, talk to me my beautiful princess.
Oh! Stay with me and have a cup of tea with me and Suzie.

Samantha Caunt (9)
St Martha's RC Primary School, Kings Lynn

Football Freak

Football freak,
The ref is a geek.

Players signing autographs,
Mostly on photographs.

Strikers scoring,
The crowd is roaring.

Norwich winning,
Wimbledon losing.

The Premiership's the best,
Non-league is the worst.

Football freak,
The ref is a geek.

Martin Gibbs (9)
St Martha's RC Primary School, Kings Lynn

Africa

In Africa where I was born,
The sun shines on the fields of corn.
The scorpions scurry in the sand,
The cheetah runs fast on land.
The monkeys swing in the trees,
And below fly the bumblebees.
The lion lays in his pack,
Tired from following the track.
The sun sets in a beautiful sky,
After the day has gone by.

Vincent Hart (9)
St Martha's RC Primary School, Kings Lynn

The Lake District

A place where history flows by,
When spirits fly over the hills,
When the scent of flowers shows power
To light memories of a great dream gone by.
Of course people are carefree
Of course people drink fresh water from the river.
Winter ruins this land but spring brings joy
To start it again.

Joel Matthews (9)
St Martha's RC Primary School, Kings Lynn

I Tried To Help Her

I tried to help her.
I couldn't help
it
She ran and ran but
fell over my
gum
Oh! Mum, what
shall I
do?

William Robinson (9)
St Martha's RC Primary School, Kings Lynn

A Dream

The drums keep the beat,
The whistle keeps the tune,
People sing under the moon,
The music, so clear, carries on all night,
The fire, so warm, is burning bright,
I'm falling asleep under the stars,
But when I wake up I hear nothing but cars.

Eleanor Smith (10)
St Martha's RC Primary School, Kings Lynn

Disasters

Disasters in pleasant boats,
Disasters in spluttering ships,
Disasters in musical notes,
Disasters in advice tips.

Disasters in roaring planes,
Disasters in high flights,
Disasters in the fast lane,
Disasters with colourful kites.

Disasters with nagging teachers,
Disasters with caring friends,
Disasters with cute creatures,
Disasters that never end.

Maria L'Estrange (10)
St Martha's RC Primary School, Kings Lynn

The Boy On The Bus

I went to the bus one morning,
The bus was really boring,
I hopped on the bus,
The driver's name was Gus,
The only seat that was free,
Was the one next to he.
He looked very unpleasant,
Rather like a pheasant,
He picked his nose,
And had horrible clothes,
And I never sat next to him again!

Lauren Rasberry (11)
St Martha's RC Primary School, Kings Lynn

The Great Players Of Liverpool

I'll start with Ian Rush,
his hair looks like a bush,
he scored lots of goals,
and he's better than Paul Scholes.

Now it's Michael Owen,
he's the best player in this poem,
he's not going to Chelsea,
people think he might be.

This time it's Harry Kewell,
he makes the opposition drool,
he wears number seven,
and when you see his dribbling, you're in Heaven.

Last but not least, it's Stevie G,
he's always hurting his knee,
he wears number seventeen,
and his favourite colour's green,
and this poem was written by me.

Daniel Cody (11)
St Martha's RC Primary School, Kings Lynn

Aston Villa

A ston Villa are cool, beating everyone,
S tars like Angel, Vassell and Dublin,
T ons of goals and cheers, hooray,
O nly Aston Villa are OK.
N o one can win when they're about,

V ultures are they, they swoop down and steal the ball,
I n and out the defenders they go,
L ike a light, like a flash,
L ike a cat they pounce, so hip, hip hooray,
A nd that's Aston Villa, they're the best overall, the best.

Ashley Sheen (11)
St Martha's RC Primary School, Kings Lynn

The Sea

The sea is a vile and dangerous place,
Yet beautiful in its own way.
The powerful waves flow and race,
As it continues its marathon day after day.

Deep under the swirling black surface,
Is hidden a stunning lagoon.
Where the fish are colourful, and flow with the sea's pace,
And the sea air above whistles a tune.

As sheets of mist blanket the water,
The sun begins to fall out of the sky.
Ships sail out of the water to take cover,
As the seagulls soar and fly high.

Carolyn Dales (11)
St Martha's RC Primary School, Kings Lynn

Night-Time

The night falls upon us,
Everywhere was silent apart from Uncle Gus,
He walked towards the dark street,
Treading slowly across the peat.
The ants and birds don't make a move,
The pavement full of grooves.
The old man staggered round that place,
Only night-time saw his face.
The old man full of grace,
The morning came and he stumbled . . .
At a slow,
        slow pace.

Carla Dye (10)
St Martha's RC Primary School, Kings Lynn

Why?

Why is the world as round as it is?
Why does the wind go by in a whizz?
Why are the clouds fluffy and white?
Why is the sky so dark at night?

Why do we have hands and feet?
Why is our skin brown or peach?
Why do we have our legs to walk?
Why do we have a voice to talk?

So many questions with no answers,
So many routines and fun dances,
One thing that is really bugging me,
Why am I waiting for answers,
    Angrily?

Samantha Harrington (11)
St Martha's RC Primary School, Kings Lynn

Dolphins

Dolphins are my favourite,
Sharks chase them, how can they take it?

They swim so gracefully,
I couldn't even swim that carefully.

Dolphins need affection,
Though we can't always give it,
So we need an affectionate invention.

They are so clever,
They deserve to live forever.

Dolphins need a rest,
They are always racing as if they are in a test.

Dolphins are my favourite,
Sharks chase them, how can they take it?

Colleen Nolan (10)
St Martha's RC Primary School, Kings Lynn

Guinea Pigs, Guinea Pigs

I am in love with guinea pigs,
Mine are Ginger, Lightning and Dwane
They are so much like little bundles of fluff
They scamper around, especially on the ground
And they like to even when there's rain.

Ginger is a pudgy pig,
Lightning is a noisy darling
And Dwane scampers around like anything
I love them so much,
Even if they are Dutch
And I will cry my eyes out when they die.

Every night they are so sweet
And they jump into their bed
Their hutch is like home
It is where they roam
And at night it tucks them up to bed.

Jessamine Hopkins (10)
St Martha's RC Primary School, Kings Lynn

The Sun

The sun is so hot and round
And always shines on the ground.

It's a great ball of fire
And really great to admire.

It shines above the meadow
And it's really, really yellow.

So bright are its rays,
Can blind you in one gaze.

It shines right through the clouds,
To make your skin a golden brown.

Holly Ambrose (10)
St Martha's RC Primary School, Kings Lynn

Chad

There once was a mouse called Chad
Who was very evil and bad
He looted his mother
Scared his brother
He was an evil lad!

That young Chad
Was getting more and more bad
Monday: scared a toad
Tuesday: blocked the road
Wednesday: he fooled the police.

Chad was a nasty piece of work
He bullied a frog called Kirk
Kirk told his mum
Chad got smacked on the bum
Then said, 'I'd better be good!'

Rebecca Leventhall (10)
St Martha's RC Primary School, Kings Lynn

The Seaside

See the sun shine on the sea,
Eagles fly past me,
As I go along the beach
See the sand on my feet,
Eagles fly to their bed
The day has gone,
Nowhere to spend.

Megan Nolan (8)
St Martha's RC Primary School, Kings Lynn

A Mother's Love

A mother's love is always genuine and true,
You give me joy, happiness and comfort each minute
Heaven sent . . .
A mother's love is always strong no matter what it takes.
Obstacles in life are always handled with love and affection.
Truly, she is always there for us in times of laughter
When we are happy, sorrow when we are sad,
Having her own problems and burdens in life,
She always keeps them aside.
Emphasising family, love and religion as her priority.
Remembering my mother's love makes her
The most wonderful person I've ever had . . .
I love you, Mama!

Melrie Antoinette A Fabian (8)
St Martha's RC Primary School, Kings Lynn

Anger - Haiku

You fight with anger,
It's like a red-hot chilli,
Your ears are steaming.

Bairavi Bala (9)
St Martha's RC Primary School, Kings Lynn

Pain - Haiku

I'm red in the face,
My head is in a big knot,
Which way should I go?

Séan McQuaid (8)
St Martha's RC Primary School, Kings Lynn

Bugs

Inside the horrid bucket there is . . .
An adding, artistic Asian ant,
A bombarding, boiling, bold butterfly,
A buzzing, bad, banging bee,
A candy-coloured, cranky cockroach,
A mummified, mad, manky millipede,
A silly, sleepy, snoring spider
Inside
    The
       Horrid
          Bucket.

Guy Williams (9)
St Martha's RC Primary School, Kings Lynn

Swimming - Haiku

Legs as a rudder,
Your arms like a propeller,
A warm, wet body.

Steven Frazer (9)
St Martha's RC Primary School, Kings Lynn

Winter - Haiku

Soft as a kitten
Bare trees dancing in the wind
Snowfall trickling down.

Kerrie Gilboy (9)
St Martha's RC Primary School, Kings Lynn

I Sense A Tear

I sense a tear trickling down
On the face without a sound.

It leaves a mark to show it's been there
The tears hide away in their little lair.

Tears are good
They're drops of joy.

I sense a tear all alone
In the corner on its own.

It needs to trickle down the face
So all your thoughts will embrace.

Josephine E Partridge (8)
St Martha's RC Primary School, Kings Lynn

A Flash Of Lightning

As the darkness loomed,
An orchestra boomed.
The drums went *thump, thump, thump,*
The cymbals crashed,
As the lightning flashed
And my heart went *pump, pump, pump.*

The horns started hooting,
The flutes started tooting
And the bells went *ding, ding, ding,*
As the saxophone swayed to the old trombone
It made me *sing, sing, sing, sing, sing, sing!*

Molly Hill (9)
St Martha's RC Primary School, Kings Lynn

Seaside - Haiku

Waves against the shore,
Sun sparkling like a gold coin,
Sand shining like jewels.

Katie Smith (8)
St Martha's RC Primary School, Kings Lynn

Arsenal

A rsenal, they completely overshadow everyone,
R eigning on their mighty throne,
S tars like Henry, Pires and Bergkamp,
E ven Toure could not stop this trio,
N ot taking drugs like Rio,
A rsenal, on this formidable run,
L ooking invincible, where will they stop?

James France (10)
St Martha's RC Primary School, Kings Lynn

Inside The Horrid Sink

Inside the horrid sink there is . . .
A silly, sleepy, snoring spider,
A cranky cockroach, creeping, criminally,
A mummified, mad, moody millipede,
A big, buzzy bee, boldly,
A drugged, droning, damp dragonfly,
Inside the horrid sink.

Sam Pressling (9)
St Martha's RC Primary School, Kings Lynn

Pirates

Skull and crossbones on the sail,
They get through every storm and hail
Drinking rum all through the night
Sometimes they have a fight.
Rotten teeth, pointy hat
Tall and thin, big and fat
Nasty minds
Lots of kinds.
Black hair
Wicked glare
Drinking rum all through the night
Sometimes they have a fight.
They get through every storm and hail
Skull and crossbones on the sail.

Emma Tilbrook (9)
St Martha's RC Primary School, Kings Lynn

Dragons - Haiku

Dragons are legends
They breathe fire over us
They are in the dark.

Jack Reed (8)
St Martha's RC Primary School, Kings Lynn

Reg Ran Round The Rugged Rock

Reg ran round the rugged rock,
He saw a sight and got a shock.
He ran back to the rock
And ran round the rugged rock.

Ella Bliss (8)
St Martha's RC Primary School, Kings Lynn

What Is Red?

Apples are redder than space rockets
When you cut your hand blood comes shooting out
Roses are as red as a vein in your hand
Flowers are as red as love hearts.
When you squash a tomato it pops
Red is like the sun in the sky
When you touch lipstick it is like a flaming sky
Books are red like shooting stars.

Victoria Wiglusz (7)
St Martha's RC Primary School, Kings Lynn

Sight

I can see a building far away
And animals that live in the distance
It's the sun, the sun
High up in the sky.

Clouds in the air
People travelling here and there
Cars whizzing by.

Trees blowing far away
You can see the hills miles away.

I can see windows
With people eating turkey.

Writing on paper
I see chairs squeaking
I see people blowing on tissues
And also I can see pencils writing.

Courtney Beales (8)
St Martha's RC Primary School, Kings Lynn

Smells

I like the smell of brand new trainers
I love the smell of polish.
I love sweets very much
They make me smile.
I hate the smell of smoke
And Uncle Kevin's cigars!
I like the smell of soap,
It makes my hands sparkle.
I love the smell of fire,
It smells like fresh bathrooms
I like the smell of sweet hay
Because it's like the countryside.
I like the smell of soup
Because it warms me inside.
I like the smell of lemon
Which is very tasty.
I love the taste and smell of melon
Which is very nice.
I especially love the scent of flowers.

Siobhan Kavanagh (7)
St Martha's RC Primary School, Kings Lynn

Winter

The snow in winter is such a wonderful sight,
It lies on the ground reflecting the light.

The wind blows with mighty force,
When I'm walking it knocks me off my course.

Sometimes in winter I feel so cold
I put on some more clothes and I look so old.

In winter you hope that spring
Is just around the corner.

Alexander Havercroft (8)
St Martha's RC Primary School, Kings Lynn

Football

I went to the football to watch my team
And when they scored I let out a scream
We all jumped up and cheered aloud
As me and my dad sat in the crowd
Our striker got fouled, he looked in pain
He took the free kick and scored again
The whistle had blown and we had won
Going to football is real good fun.

Marcus Ashley (11)
St Michael's VA Middle School, Bowthorpe

My Fish

(But what do they do in the water?)

My fish are cool,
But what do they do in the water?

Do they . . .
Sit and play chess all day long?

My fish are excellent at eating,
But what do they do in the water?

Do they . . .
Go to school?

That's what I want to find out!

Casey Quadling (10)
St Michael's VA Middle School, Bowthorpe

Football

Football is a game
Jake is my name
I play for Jex
Saving all the balls.

My best friend Jack
He runs like a cheetah
Scoring all the goals
Whizzing past the keeper
One more time
We won again.

Jake Armes (10)
St Michael's VA Middle School, Bowthorpe

My Baby Cousin

My baby cousin
Is so sweet,
He is warm and cuddly,
I want him all for me,
He's my baby cousin.

My baby cousin,
Is like red and white roses
And sweet buttercups,
Better than better itself,
He's my baby cousin.

My baby cousin,
He likes me,
His smile is lovely,
I love him so much,
He's my baby cousin.

Georgia Heggie (11)
St Michael's VA Middle School, Bowthorpe

The Curtains

(In the style of Miroslav Holub)

Pull open the curtains,
Maybe there's a field full of leprechauns,
To make your dreams come true,
Or lovely little fairies,
Playing with butterflies.

Pull open the curtains,
Maybe there's a garden,
Full of gorgeous, flower fragrances,
Lots of different kinds of blossom,
Some wild, some tropical and maybe exotic.

Pull open the curtains,
Maybe there's a white wolf,
On top of the cold mountain,
Or a hot, stripy, bothered tiger,
Waiting for lunch.

Pull open the curtains,
Maybe there's a thick layer of snow,
Or maybe a hot desert,
Full of snakes,
Wriggling and slithering about.

Pull open the curtains,
Maybe there's a pair of white, beautiful doves,
Hovering in the blue sky,
Or a brown, furry squirrel,
Crunching a crispy hazelnut.
Pull open the curtains!

Farah Nizal (9)
St Michael's VA Middle School, Bowthorpe

The Door

(Based on 'The Door' by Miroslav Holub)

Go and open the door
Maybe there are boys playing football in the yard
Or a rainbow falling to the ground.

Go and open the door
Maybe there's a kitten behind the door
Or a cat and dog waiting for a bus at a lamp post.

Go and open the door
Maybe there's a teacher with my friends
Or a man swimming.

Go and open the door
Maybe there are three teenagers
Or dolphins in the sea.

Go and open the door
Maybe there is my mum and dad, brothers and sister
Waiting for me, or a large lid.

Go and open the door
Maybe there's a chair for me to sit on
Or two boys singing.

Go and open the door
Maybe there is a girl laughing
Or girls and boys skipping by a golden tree.

Kelly Crome (8)
St Michael's VA Middle School, Bowthorpe

Love

She is a caring person,
She smells like a rose,
She's as beautiful as a butterfly,
She's always there when you're alone,
She's as sweet as a flower
And sings sweetly to you.
       That's *love!*

Jasmine Crotch (10)
St Michael's VA Middle School, Bowthorpe

Open The Door

(Based on 'The Door' by Miroslav Holub)

Open the door
maybe you'll find
a footballer kicking
a football.

Open the door
maybe you'll find
a large jewel
glowing like the sun.

Open the door
maybe you'll find
1,000 doors
as big as you.

Open the door
maybe you'll find
your favourite chocolate
as big as your school.

Callum Smith (8)
St Michael's VA Middle School, Bowthorpe

Open The Door

(Based on 'The Door' by Miroslav Holub)

Go and open the door
Step into the future fantasy
Flying cars go whizzing by.

Go and open the door
You might see a running tree
Or ducks hooting, 'Goodbye, goodbye.'

Go and open the door
Dinosaurs eating mud like ice cream
Yum, yum and yum.

Jake Cranston (9)
St Michael's VA Middle School, Bowthorpe

The Door
(Based on 'The Door' by Miroslav Holub)

Go and open the door
You could find three black penguins.

Go and open the door
Maybe you'll find seven dwarves standing in a row.

Go and open the door
You'll find ten flying pigs floating up in the air.

Go and open the door
You might find a postman standing on the wall.

Go and open the door
You might find ten men marching to the post office.

Go and open the door
You might find six balls bouncing up and down.

Go and open the door
You might find a donkey standing on a car.

Go and open the door
You might find two massive books as big as your house.

Go and open the door
You might find smelly roses and blossoms.

Luke Goodswen (8)
St Michael's VA Middle School, Bowthorpe

In War

There he lay, helpless and defenceless,
His eyes watering from the gas.
He couldn't breathe
He couldn't call for help, no one would hear anyway
He looked at the injury on his leg
He just wished he was dead
The pain was unbearable
The noise deafening
He had no hope in the world.
That is war.

John Chapman (11)
St Michael's VA Middle School, Bowthorpe

The Door

(Based on 'The Door' by Miroslav Holub)

Go and open the door.
There's a pop star at your door
singing your favourite song
or a bird that will peck off your nose.

> Go and open the door.
> There's a big lion there,
> surprisingly he's smiling at you
> and gives you a big kiss.

Go and open the door.
Your door is full of snow
and there's a green alien
wearing glasses.

Nikita Bilham (9)
St Michael's VA Middle School, Bowthorpe

Disneyland

D isney dollars
I magination
S urprises on the way
N ightly performances
E normous buffets
Y our dream come true
L azy river
A utographs of Disney characters
N ail-biting roller coasters
D elicious desserts.

Alice Dover (11)
St Michael's VA Middle School, Bowthorpe

The Curtains

(In the style of Miroslav Holub)

Pull open the curtains,
Maybe there's a golden sunshine,
A thunderstorm
Or a snow spell.

Pull open the curtains,
Maybe there's a lion sleeping,
A rhino charging at its enemy,
Or birds communicating to others.

Pull open the curtains,
Maybe there's a hornet eating its enemy,
Baby eggs of a butterfly hatching,
Or ants running around.

Pull open the curtains,
Maybe there's a crystal panther,
A silver cheetah
Or a golden baby cub as shiny as 24 carat gold.

Joshua Moore (8)
St Michael's VA Middle School, Bowthorpe

Mini Rugby

We play on a Sunday
With training when there is no match
We pass from side to side
Backwards, never forwards,
We score a try but never a conversion
Here comes a scrum, mind your head
One day I'll play for England
Got to work hard.
Hooray we've won the match!

Iain Savage (10)
St Michael's VA Middle School, Bowthorpe

A Polar Bear

The big, white polar bear
Jumping in the snow
The moonlight shines on his fur
The fur twinkles like the stars
With his big eyes
And his big, wet nose
He smells the fish
Swimming in the pool
He puts his nose in the water
Pulls out a big fish
Oh what a lovely, cuddly,
Big, white polar bear.

Craig Turner (10)
St Michael's VA Middle School, Bowthorpe

The Curtains

(In the style of Miroslav Holub)

Pull open the curtains,
Maybe there's a rainbow,
With gold at the end,
Maybe there's a sports car,
Waiting to be used.

Pull open the curtains,
Maybe there's a perfect world,
Where cats and dogs are friends,
Or no humans are bad.

Pull open the curtains,
Maybe there's a tidal wave of friendship,
Waiting to be spread.

Josh Bugg (9)
St Michael's VA Middle School, Bowthorpe

Friendship - Emotions

Friendship trusts me always, no matter what I do!
She trusts me when I lie, she trusts me with the truth.

Friendship trusts me, she always plays with me,
No matter how nasty I am!
Friendship never buys me presents
But it's better to give than to receive.

Even when Friendship cries,
She'll still have me by her side.

That's Friendship.

Jade Hudson (10)
St Michael's VA Middle School, Bowthorpe

The Curtains

(In the style of Miroslav Holub)

Pull open the curtains,
Maybe there's a cave,
Full of treasure and golden money,
Or a magical tunnel.

Pull open the curtains,
Maybe there's a mythical castle,
Sparkling silver and gold turrets,
Or a turquoise-blue pond,
With slippery dolphins diving!

Lauren Bunn (9)
St Michael's VA Middle School, Bowthorpe

The Curtains

(In the style of Miroslav Holub)

Pull open the curtains,
Maybe there's a peaceful waterfall,
Or a colourful rainbow,
Maybe there's a golden sunshine.

Pull open the curtains,
Maybe there's a crystal panther,
Or a platinum dragon,
Maybe there's a golden lion.

Will Chapman (8)
St Michael's VA Middle School, Bowthorpe

The Curtains

(In the style of Miroslav Holub)

Pull open the curtains,
Maybe there's a thunderstorm,
Or rain or sunshine,
Maybe there's a snowstorm.

Pull open the curtains,
Maybe there's a butterfly,
Or a squirrel or an ant,
Maybe you'll see a giraffe.

James Frost (8)
St Michael's VA Middle School, Bowthorpe

Dragons

Red and glistening in the dark
Living in an ancient ark
Living in a pack of four
With a really damp and creaky floor
Dark and dingy is the night
Added to a nasty fright
Keep my words that I shall say
Be careful or you will pay.

Bethany Howard (10)
St Michael's VA Middle School, Bowthorpe

The Curtains
(In the style of Miroslav Holub)

Pull open the curtains,
Maybe there's a hailstorm,
With hail as big as watermelons,
Or a lightning storm or maybe snow.

Pull open the curtains,
Maybe there's a grave,
Or a set of Roman armour,
Or perhaps a skeleton in the armour.

Pull open the curtains,
Maybe there's a trench,
Or a motorbike,
There might be a fighter plane,
Firing at another fighter plane.

Thomas Davies (8)
St Michael's VA Middle School, Bowthorpe

The Curtains
(In the style of Miroslav Holub)

Pull open the curtains,
There may be a cottage.

Pull open the curtains,
There may be a lake.

Pull open the curtains,
There may be a lion.

Pull open the curtains,
It might be snowing.

Pull open the curtains,
It might be dark.

Sophie Bush (8)
St Michael's VA Middle School, Bowthorpe

The Curtains

(In the style of Miroslav Holub)

Pull open the curtains,
Maybe outside there's a bird or two,
A squirrel,
Or a dog running.

Pull open the curtains,
Maybe there's a snowman
Running down the road,
Or the sun shining.

Pull open the curtains,
If there's a face,
Close them!

Charley Barker (8)
St Michael's VA Middle School, Bowthorpe

The Curtains

(In the style of Miroslav Holub)

Pull open the curtains,
Maybe there's a colourful rainbow,
With gold at the end,
A crystal maze,
Or a jewel-making factory.

Pull open the curtains,
Maybe there's a friendly world,
Where dogs and cats make friends
And no humans can be nasty.

Antonio Wedral (8)
St Michael's VA Middle School, Bowthorpe

The Curtains

(In the style of Miroslav Holub)

Pull open the curtains,
Maybe there are trees waving,
Shaking in the cold,
Or a melting snowman.

Pull open the curtains,
Maybe there's snow,
Falling from the sky,
Or a warm, sunny day.

Matthew Manning (9)
St Michael's VA Middle School, Bowthorpe

The Curtains

(In the style of Miroslav Holub)

Pull open the curtains,
Maybe there's a teleporting archer,
Or an invisible man with a walking stick.

Pull open the curtains,
Maybe there's a tornado,
A blizzard,
Or a cascade of rain.

Jacob Pearson (9)
St Michael's VA Middle School, Bowthorpe

The Curtains

(In the style of Miroslav Holub)

Pull open the curtains,
Maybe there's a robin,
A gang of bats,
Or a weeping willow.

Pull open the curtains,
Maybe there's a big dog with red, steaming eyes,
Or a snowman twitching one eye,
Or a cat miaowing at the cold swimming pool.

Ashleigh Felstead White (9)
St Michael's VA Middle School, Bowthorpe

The Curtains

(In the style of Miroslav Holub)

Pull open the curtains,
Maybe there's a snowstorm,
Or a golden, glowing sun,
Or maybe a big swimming pool.

Pull open the curtains,
Maybe there is a dark forest,
Or lovely bunches of flowers,
Or maybe a dirty, dark swamp.

Pull open the curtains,
Maybe there'll be a lovely pair of doves,
Or a land full of animals
And a big tiger.

Pull open the curtains,
Maybe there'll be a world full of birds.

Shannon Vince (9)
St Michael's VA Middle School, Bowthorpe

The Curtains

(In the style of Miroslav Holub)

Pull open the curtains,
Maybe there's a flowing river of chocolate,
Or a magic rainbow.

Pull open the curtains,
Maybe there's a three-eyed fish that grants wishes
Or a frog that grows flowers.

Pull open the curtains,
Maybe there's a magic school with golden children.

Robert George (9)
St Michael's VA Middle School, Bowthorpe

The Curtains
(In the style of Miroslav Holub)

Pull open the curtains,
Maybe there's a mad professor,
Made of chocolate candyfloss,
Or a caramel lake.
Pull open the curtains,
Maybe there's a candy lolly,
Waiting for a lick.
Pull open the curtains,
Maybe there's a hideous ghost,
Waiting for you to be horrified.

Ryan Jones (8)
St Michael's VA Middle School, Bowthorpe

The Curtains
(In the style of Miroslav Holub)

Pull open the curtains,
Maybe there's a sports car,
Or a big lorry,
Revving its engine.

Pull open the curtains,
Maybe there's a cave,
Full of sparkly treasures,
Or a disgusting bat.

Christopher Kinnier (9)
St Michael's VA Middle School, Bowthorpe

Wintertime

It is winter like it is every year.
Frost and wind and it is dark.
My father lights the fire every single year.
I love the year.

Eleanor Brighton (7)
St Nicholas House School, North Walsham

Tom's Kenning

I'm a . . .

football player
moody teenager
goal stopper
PlayStation 2 player
music lover
teasing brother
door shutter
sleepy sleeper
hard worker
fishy swimmer
demon texter
avid reader.

Joe Annison (8)
St Nicholas House School, North Walsham

The Sea

S ee the beach, see the sea, it is so pretty.
E ach day the sea crashes endlessly into the shore
A lways washing the pebbles and sand crystal clean
S ometimes the waves are really big, they crash into the cliff
H ow powerful the sea can be when it's angry
O r how tranquil and soothing it can be
R eally when it's calm and still it is a thing of beauty
E veryone can sit and dream and enjoy its mystery.

Alexander Whitbread (10)
St Nicholas House School, North Walsham

Anonymous

I'm anonymous
But you should find out who, if you follow my clues,
I live by the seaside in very hot climates,
My feet are built into the sand,
My trunk is brown and I grow green hair,
When it is hot you will thank me for shelter,
I am, as you might have guessed, a palm tree.

Joe Oakey (10)
St Nicholas House School, North Walsham

Snowballs

S now is falling
N o rainy showers, hip hip hooray
O utside it is snowing hard
W hite, fluffy, cold snow has come at last
B alls of snow to throw
A nimals hibernating in cracks
L ight has faded in the winter nights
L ovely snowmen standing in gardens
S nowmen standing straight and tall.

Madeline Buxton (9)
St Nicholas House School, North Walsham

Winter

Dark nights, gloomy nights, cold nights
Winds so bitter, frostbite on your toes
Coughs and splutters, sneezes and colds
Frost gleaming in the sun like diamonds on a string.

Annabel Crane (8)
St Nicholas House School, North Walsham

In The Ocean

As I jump into the sea
All the rock pool life swims around me
As I swim into the ocean
My frog legs kick in a peculiar motion
Killer whales, dolphins, fish
None of them a tasty dish
Scary sharks and crabs around me
I found this world or it found me
I see a wonderful coral reef
Each piece as delicate as a leaf
Pink and purple, greeny trees
Living under raging seas
But then my tank runs out of air
And I haven't got an air tank spare.

Elliott Palmer (10)
St Nicholas House School, North Walsham

Apple Crumble

A pple crumble is delicious
P eople always eat apple crumble
P erhaps farmers' tummies are rumblous
L ong and thin apple crumble is divine
E very crumble is heavenly

C runchy apple crumble is lovely
R umble in my tum
U nderneath is apple
M unchy crumble
B eautiful stuff it is
L ovely it is and loads of crumble
E lephants always like apple crumble.

Luke Robson (9)
St Nicholas House School, North Walsham

A Poem About The Sea

We went to the beach, it was a very sunny day
And I found a pebble in a rock pool not far away
I picked up the pebble and twisted it in my hand,
I showed it to Mum who threw it back on the sand.

I ran back to the pool and do you know what I found?
A massive crab sitting there right in the sand!
The crab looked at me and I looked at it,
Then off it scuttled and buried itself in a pit.

I looked for just a little bit more,
There was seaweed and shells strewn across the floor,
The seaweed was squishy, smelly and cool,
I soon threw that back into the pool.

I collected the shells that laid about,
They were pretty and were once a nice home, no doubt!
I put the shells into the pocket of my coat,
'No, no, no,' said Mum, 'please not your coat.'

I emptied out the shells and placed them in a row,
Then I decided which ones I should keep and which ones should go.
I ended up with five, big ones, if you must know,
I sneaked them in my pocket, Mum would never know.

Dad started to call, 'Let's go home,'
We walked towards the car feeling sad because we had to go.
We drove off sadly watching the beach fall behind,
Feeling that was the saddest time today.

Charlotte Bacon (9)
St Nicholas House School, North Walsham

Snowball

S now is falling all is white
N ow we are playing snowballs
O utside it is now white
W e can all build a snowman
B uild a wall of snow
A ll children are outside playing in snow
L ots of snow will soon be gone
L ots of fires being lit
S now we hope will come again.

Henry Harrison (10)
St Nicholas House School, North Walsham

Winter Poem

S now in the garden
N ow it's all around
O n the roof the snow is there
W ith the frozen ice
B lizzards and brightness all around
A ll the snow is dropping with no single sound
L ots of snow is around, now let's go and play
L et's go and play in the snow while it's still there
S ome ice is thin and some ice is thick.

Henry Hale (9)
St Nicholas House School, North Walsham

Winter Poem

Frost on the cars, sparkling in the moonlight
Ice forming on the road
Stars burning in the sky
I sneeze in bed and fall asleep
Wondering what I will do tomorrow.

Miles Hodges (8)
St Nicholas House School, North Walsham

The Snowstorm

S now is falling out of the sky
N o one knows the secrets
O utside
W indy hail
B lizzards all around
A ll that is left is one flower
L ifeless snow
L ifeless play
S now is all around, let's play.

Alice Harvey (9)
St Nicholas House School, North Walsham

Snow Poem

S now is falling, snow on snow
N ow children play
O utside the snow is silvery white
W hile footsteps lay on the ground
B uild a snowman higher and higher
A ll the snowflakes are falling lower and lower
L ittle cars are getting stuck
L ight of the moon is coming out
S now is the best time of the year.

Henry Dewing (10)
St Nicholas House School, North Walsham

The Snowstorm

S now has now fallen
N ow it is white
O n the roads the ice is quite thick
W hiter than white.
B righter than sky
A ll is quite merry
L ots of snow
L ots of children
S now is now melting, enjoy it while you can.

John Neville (11)
St Nicholas House School, North Walsham

A Winter Poem

S now is falling all around
N ow all is white
O utdoors is a new world
W here all is cold and bright
B ut good for snowmen
A nd sledging too
L ong as you wrap up warm
L egs, arms and body
S now will be your friend.

Emily Gair (10)
St Nicholas House School, North Walsham

Ice Cream

I ce cream is delicious
C andy is nice
E veryone likes ice cream

C hocolate is yummy
R eading makes me sick because I don't like reading
E very Friday I eat chocolate at school
A lot of ice cream makes me happy
M um tells me don't eat a lot of sweet things.

Hazel Cheung (11)
St Nicholas House School, North Walsham

Chicken Soup

C hicken soup is very nice
H ow can you not like chicken soup?
I like chicken soup
C hicken soup is my favourite soup because it is English
K etchup doesn't go with chicken soup
E at chicken soup to warm you up
N o one likes ice-cold chicken soup

S oup is nice
O ur soups are best
U se chicken to make the soup
P eople like chicken soup.

Ben Brighton (10)
St Nicholas House School, North Walsham

Magical May

Magical May with stars at night,
Magical May with moon so bright.

Magical May with lots of sun,
Magical May come, come, come.

Magical May come and see,
Magical May come with me!

Adam Nelson (10)
Saxlingham Primary School

The Lioness' Big Secret!

She walks around with a big plump belly,
Her friends all think it's too much jelly,
But the greatest thing is,
Nobody knows,
What's really growing in that belly of hers!

As she slithers through the darkness,
When everyone's asleep,
She lays down
Then *pop!* She sees eight little feet,
The annnoying thing now is,
She has *two little lion cubs to feed!*

Lucie Santander (10)
Saxlingham Primary School

Bullet

A steel dart flying through the air,
Comes speeding out of its metal lair,
She moves like a small cloud with the wind,
Representing a person who has sinned,
Hitting the victim with a thud,
The sound of the victim in the mud.

Kingsley J White (10)
Saxlingham Primary School

Oddums

A pin has a head, but no hair,
A clock a face, but no nose there.
A needle has an eye, but does not see,
A river runs, but not like me.
A sea has a bed, but not a sheet,
A hill has a foot, not some feet.
Ash trees have keys, but never a lock,
A saw has teeth, but does not mock.
And in this world we are leaning,
On the words with different meanings.

Alfie Chapman (11)
Saxlingham Primary School

Labradors

Labradors are black
Labradors are yellow
Labradors are brown
And have a little frown

Labradors are playful
Labradors are sleepy
Labradors are hungry
And they like to hunt

Labradors are cute
Labradors are lovely
Labradors are fluffy
And always lay down

Labradors are good
Labradors are friendly
Labradors are big
And they are full of fun!

James Chadwick (10)
Saxlingham Primary School

The Lion And The Mouse

Squeak, squeak!
Nibble, nibble!
Rummage, rummage!
Pitter-patter!
Pitter-patter!
Pitter . . .
Eeeek!
Oh! No, no, no, no, no
I'll do anything you want only if you
Stop chasing me please!
Oh! Mr Lion are you caught in a net?
Are you tricked or trapped?
Do not worry I will get you out
And be free just like me.
There you go, you are free
I just don't want to be thanked.
Squeak, squeak!
Nibble, nibble!
Rummage, rummage!
Pitter-patter!
Pitter-patter!
Pitter-patter pit!
Eeeeekkkk!

Holly Flegg (10)
Saxlingham Primary School

Winter

W arm is lovely when you're cold
 I ce creeps across the pond
N ice, you make a snowman bold
T weeting birds are getting frozen
E ver-ending icicles you hold
R ight away you go away, waiting for the snow to play.

James Burrough (8)
Saxlingham Primary School

A Dirty Washing Poem

Washing, washing with a boom and a bang,
Wallop and a crash
And lots and lots of bundles of clothes
On the odd-looking floor,
Sounds like the speed of a roller coaster,
Hissing like the sound of a snake,
In the cauldron that is spinning round.
Never does it stop whirling and twirling round,
Going round like a car going round a track.

Gregory Edwards (9)
Saxlingham Primary School

My Elephant

I love my elephant with an E.
He is enormous.
He lives in England.
He will get exhausted when he runs.
Embarrassed when he's on show.
He has enormous eyes.
He eats anything.
He will even eat electricity.
He will find it easy to impress you.
His name is Elly.
He will feel empty inside.
He sounds like he has an error
Inside him.

Caitlin Stone (8)
Saxlingham Primary School

Kittens

They fiddle they play
They giggle they sleep
When they wake up
They play with feet
They drink milk
They eat their tuna
They're small and soft
They get wet in rain and snow
And they get very dirty.

Daniel Burlingham (9)
Saxlingham Primary School

My Parrot

I love my parrot with a P
His name is pickles
He is pink and purple
He lives in Portugal
He eats pasta and pellets
He peers through his cage and
He puffs like a ball.

Claudia May St Quintin (8)
Saxlingham Primary School

Grandad Pete

My grandad Pete of Carrow Road
Has seven dogs as brown as mud
Who sit on his colossal chair
And watch Sky Sports while licking hair
They scratch their fleas and crunch and chew
Their squeaky toys white, red and blue
They bark (while watching City play)
And jump up when they score away!

John Reeve (8)
Saxlingham Primary School

Dirty Washing

When my washing is dirty
I wash it very clean
I wash it so it smells nice
Then it's a wonderful scene.

When my washing is spotless
I make it filthy again,
I made it dirty by . . .
A tomato ketchup stain.

Zachary Nelson (8)
Saxlingham Primary School

My Washing Poem

My mum does the washing every day
She does it really low
The clothes get soggy
It gets wet
It spins round and round in circles
Really fast
When we get it out
It is soggy
All the clothes go
On the washing line.

Charlie Chadwick (8)
Saxlingham Primary School

Snake

The snake slithers, it makes you shiver.
When you see their fangs, your heart goes bang.
You might think it will use them to impale *you!*
He is covered in scale, from head to tail.
When you see his forked tongue, you'd better move
But don't always think you have to.
Snake won't hurt you, so don't quake.

Jarrod Stone (9)
Saxlingham Primary School

Crime Don't Pay (If You've Got A Robot)

Jake had a plan to blow up the bank
But Robotroy's mind was really blank
Jake was a robber who had a crafty mind
Robotroy couldn't do it because he was kind.

Jake was getting the dynamite for the start
But Robotroy was getting the flight for his dart
Jake was very angry and chained him to the bike
Which Robotroy didn't like and wanted a fight.

Jake was packing up the stuff
While Robotroy had a handcuff
Everything was on the blue car
But Robotroy was still at the bar.

Jake was the dynamiter
Robotroy had the lighter
Bang, bang, bang! The dynamite is off.

There was a surrounding light
Which was very bright
Jake was arrested
Robotroy was not.

Mark Goddard (10)
Shelton With Hardwick Community School

The Sheep Can't Change!

Mummies like to fall to bits
Tudors like beheading
King John liked collecting tax
But sheep just don't like shedding

The Beatles like to play their songs
And Elvis likes to jazz
But if you say shear a sheep
They'll all be gone in a flash

The Romans liked to fight all day
Caesar's going to burst
The only way to shear a sheep
Is to kill it first

But now things are different
Blair always gets the blame
And although Hitler's long gone
The sheep are just the same.

Jake Atherall (10)
Shelton With Hardwick Community School

Down In The Countryside

Down in the countryside
There lived a lovely girl,
Who had a fluffy stuffed dog,
Who was her favourite toy,
And everywhere she went she
Took Fluffy with her
Her biggest wish was that
It was a real dog friend.

One day she was pretending
To take it for a walk,
Then it came alive,
She was really shocked,
She carried on the walk,
Until she got to the wonderful
Supermarket.

She met a handsome boy
Who saw the lovely dog,
He saw the dog's leg move,
He knew it was alive,
They kept it as a secret,
They had a real dog friend.

Chloe Loftus (8)
Shelton With Hardwick Community School

Uncle Nick

At the great white house my uncle Nick
Got out of bed and grabbed a stick
He knocked out the guards
And climbed up the drain
Then he had a good look around
And climbed down again

The very next night he climbed out of bed
'It's time to steal the bank,' he said
He got the bank
And drove it away
But then the police caught
Him the very next day

He escaped from the jail by burning the door
He stepped into a passage and through a trapdoor
He landed on a jailer
And knocked him out cold
So Uncle left the jail
Feeling very bold

My uncle Nick then stole a flan to help him think another plan
And when he had, off he went to electrify the president!
He put the batteries near a shop
Full of fireworks to the top
But in his plan
Something went wrong
There was a big bang
And Uncle had gone.

Joseph Sieveking (10)
Shelton With Hardwick Community School

Tiger One Tiger Two

Tiger one
Tiger two
Tiger jump
To the zoo

Rabbit three
Rabbit four
Rabbit hop
Through the door

Lion five
Lion six
Lion break
All the sticks

Piggy seven
Piggy eight
Piggy eat
Off the plate

Horsey nine
Horsey ten
Why is Horsey using
My whiteboard pen?

Madeline Tyler (8)
Shelton With Hardwick Community School

She Rapped At The Shop

(Based on 'Gran Can You Rap?' by Jack Ousbey)

She rapped at the shop and to the staff.
She rapped past the jokes and she had a great laugh.
She rapped by the crisps and by the Coke
And gave a customer a great poke.
I'm the best rapping gran this world's ever seen,
I'm a hip hop, tip top, rap rap queen.

She rapped at the officer and he took her to the pub.
She rapped at a silly old man who was sitting in his chair
And she rapped at the side of his old juicy pear.
I'm the best rapping gran this world's ever seen.
I'm a mip mop, rip rap, rap nap queen.

Jessica Hoskins (10)
Shelton With Hardwick Community School

What Is Brown?

What is brown?
A tree is brown sitting in the ground.
What is grey?
A brick is grey sitting in a building.
What is yellow?
The sun is yellow sitting in the sky.
What is blue?
A pond is blue sitting in the hole.
What is red?
A tomato is red sitting on a branch.
What is green?
A pear is green sitting in a tree.

Ellen Goddard (8)
Shelton With Hardwick Community School

Babies

Baby one
Baby two
What is baby doing
In Papa's shoe?

Baby three
Baby four
What's baby doing
Shouting, 'Encore!'

Baby five
Baby six
What's baby doing
With firewood sticks?

Baby seven
Baby eight
Baby smashing
My good plate!

Natalie Sieveking (8)
Shelton With Hardwick Community School

My Fairy

I saw something move.
I saw something fly and thought it was a butterfly.
It looked like a butterfly flying by.
It was fast and slow, it was horrible.
It makes me feel sick, it makes me feel dizzy,
I turned around and by the way my name is Lizzy.
Her hair is like gold.
Her wings are like the moonlight and her eyes are brighter
Than the light.
Her dresses are pink as a rose and her lips are pink too.
Her skin is bright then white.
She has long hair like me and I like it.
I kept her and named her Bright, like the moonlight.

Stefany Barham (10)
Weasenham VC Primary School

The Dwarf

Yesterday I had an adventure
It really was terribly weird
When I told my best friend
All he did was leered
In my adventure I thought I heard
A-clinking and a-clashing
I went round a corner and there I saw
A dwarf and rocks he was a-bashing
His pick gleamed in the light of the lantern
Like a knight wielding a sword
The rubies and emeralds that he was mining
Were definitely fit for a lord
The bell on his hat jingled madly
He grunted with effort and sweat
I kept on wanting to speak to him
But my mind kept on saying *not yet*
I fell over and cut my knee
The pain was especially bad
The dwarf immediately looked up from his work
I could see he was really mad
I was so scared I could not speak
I ran and I ran down the road
Until I came to my high street
And opened the door to my abode.

Duncan Butler (9)
Weasenham VC Primary School

I Saw A Mountain Troll

I saw a mountain troll one night
It took the tree like a breeze
Its bumps were like lumps
It smelt like two eggs on legs
It can lift a car up very far
I sneaks up to the house like a mouse.

James Cruise (9)
Weasenham VC Primary School

Dryad Dance

I dreamed I saw a dryad
dancing around the trees
her flat green emerald hair
floated on the breeze

Her lips as red as rubies
her face as white as snow
then she stopped her dancing
and jumped onto a doe

The doe ran away
she ran from the wood
the dryad shouted as you would

Then the picture faded
it faded very fast
I wish I could go back
back into the past.

Harriett Spall (10)
Weasenham VC Primary School

Fee, Fie, Foe, Fum

I dreamt I saw a giant
In a cave by the sea
He hissed and hissed
But it didn't scare me
His feet were like boulders
And large pancake hands
His head sunk in his shoulders
With his hair up in bands.

Ben Dawes (10)
Weasenham VC Primary School

Pixie Polka

I thought I saw a pixie sweeping through the trees,
Her hair was like the autumn leaves flowing in the breeze.

Her bangles and earrings jingled and were studded with clean glass,
I thought I saw a glint of gold they must be made of brass.

Her trousers flew behind her flowing with fire,
It was easy to admire,
Her top was shocking green and incredibly clean.

The only thing I didn't like was her laugh like a witch's cackle,
Unfortunately then she probably went back to her gigantic castle.

Imogen Matthews (10)
Weasenham VC Primary School

The Fairy

When I was out in the woods,
I went to look for berries,
For Mummy said I could,
Get lots and lots of cherries.

When I was near the bush,
I started to pick,
But then I froze,
Because there was a prick.

A prick I thought,
Cherries don't have pricks,
So I took another look,
When I saw what it was I let out a gasp very quick.

For it was a fairy,
It was not scary,
She was just sitting there waving,
'I knew it was a fairy,' I said to myself.

Naomi Beardsley Best (9)
Weasenham VC Primary School

The Mermaid

A tail like a fish,
Tail all gold and silver,
Eyes as blue as sea,
Arm as pale as can be,
Hair as gold as silver twinkling in the air,
Her hair is very rare.

Lips as red as a rose,
Wouldn't I love a pair of those,
Scales like seashells,
Shining like Christmas bells,
Her eyes twinkle like a star,
She swims very, very far.

She sits on rocks to catch the sun,
Sometimes until the day is done,
Her hair streams like seaweed in the waves,
Her friends, the seals, watch from caves,
She swims with fishes in the water so blue,
How I wish I was a mermaid too.

Ira Everett
Weasenham VC Primary School

Dreaming Of The Mermaid

I dreamt I saw a mermaid,
Diving into the sea,
Her hair is like the golden sun,
I hide behind a big huge rock in case she may see me.
Her eyes are as green as the Barrier Reef,
She's just swam past me, what a relief.
Her belly top is as purple as the purple-headed mountain
There is a race on and I think she wants to win.

Millie Baker Lynch (7)
Weasenham VC Primary School

Minotaur

I saw a minotaur prowling in a wood
Grand horns upon his head
Then a man came running by with a black hood
A sheep lay sound asleep with old ted
The smell of the sheep led the Minotaur back to the wood.

Howls and roars came from the old oak trees
A great stone hammer lay upon a rock
Minotaur ran behind him followed by lots of killer bees
He moaned and moaned.

He fought away the bees with ease
His hammer grasped in his hands
The Minotaur walked to the beach
That was the last of Minotaurs walking along the sand.

Stewart Junior Bell (10)
Weasenham VC Primary School

Ogre Poem

I dreamt I saw an ogre,
He smelt like a dyke,
I saw him with his girlfriend,
She was riding a bike.
Then hunters came yesterday,
I watched as he drifted away,
Drifted as slow as a tiger
Which creeps on its prey.

I visited his girlfriend the next night,
I stayed for tea which filled her with delight.
I had to go but she got snappy,
So I stayed late to make her happy.
I left dream world when I woke up,
But strangely I could taste ketchup.

Kyle Watts (10)
Weasenham VC Primary School

Merman

I saw a merman in the sea
And it looked at me with a cup of tea.

I had spiky hair as green as a pear
Its scales were fair.

Its flipper made him older and he ate a kipper.

Sophie Newton (9)
Weasenham VC Primary School

My Garden Fairy

I was walking in my garden one day
When I saw something flutter by
When I saw it up close I didn't know what to say
But I thought it was a butterfly.

Its wings were tiny and small
And its hair was as yellow as the glistening sun
Its head was the size of a ping-pong ball
It was so so pretty I didn't even run.

It wasn't exactly tall but it was definitely very small
Her wings were as white as the moon
Her dress was fit for a ball
And she told me she had to go soon

So out of my hand she flew
She said she wanted to see me again
I wanted to see her again too
But then I thought are there any fairy men?

Georgia Large (9)
Weasenham VC Primary School

I Saw A Mountain Troll

I saw a mountain troll one night
He had green skin and it smelt like rotten eggs
His eyes were as green as a pear
His feet were as big as his leap
He smashed
Down pubs with his clubs
And drank out of tubs and ate cubs
His hair was very fair
And he could eat pears.

Jake Rimmer (8)
Weasenham VC Primary School

Life As A Country Child

I hate helping on the farm
Once I nearly broke my arm.
Lots of hard work to do, so little time
I've got to milk the cows at half-past nine
Then all should be fine.
But at half-past ten I've got to feed the hen.
Then I've got to collect the eggs
Then it's time to make some bread.
Now I've got a pain in my head.
12.00 it's time for lunch
We're such an unhappy bunch.
At 1.00 time to plough the fields
To get the land ready for harvest meals.
At 2.30 still lots of things to do
I have to visit the blacksmith to change the horse's shoe.
Still it's nearly time for tea
A jam sandwich for me.
Now it is nine-thirty - time for bed
Now I can rest that pain in my head.

Scott Dack (11)
Woodland View Middle School

Life On The Farm

Tired -
Don't like getting up in the dark.
I feed the pigs
I milk the cows,
It's all work, work, work.

Cold -
It's breakfast at last, bacon and bread.
Feed the ducks and geese
Fetch the eggs
It's all work, work, work.

Aching -
Up and down the field with the plough
It's time to do the threshing.
When the threshing's finished
The excitement has gone
It's all work, work, work.

Hate -
Hate weeding
Hate picking stones
Don't really like topping and tailing
It's all work, work, work.

Like -
Like to go to the blacksmith
Pumping the bellows is OK
I help to make the horses' shoes
I want to be a blacksmith
It's all work, work, work.

Life on the farm is harder than you think
Some things can be fun
Some things can be dull
It's all rush, rush, rush,
It's all work, work, work.

Georgia Livock (10)
Woodland View Middle School

I Watch The Floating Stars

I watch the floating stars go by
Way up high in the sky,
From the Earth I live on
I count them one by one,
The planets Saturn, Neptune, Pluto and Mars
Moving up there with the stars,
Then there's Uranus, Jupiter, Venus and the sun
Hot and round like a burning bun,
My favourite is Saturn
Surrounded by rings of beautiful colour,
So far away you cannot see it from the Earth -
The planet where we were born.

Francesca Cullum (9)
Woodland View Middle School

My Firework Poem

F ireworks flicker and sparkle when they explode
I t looks so pretty when they go up in the sky
R attling, startling them when they go
E xciting when they burst they give a loud bang
W hooshing, bashing, turning, whirling
O ut comes the big one, it is so scary
R acing to the sky it bangs, booms
K illing each other as they play
S parkling, shattering all over the place.

Emma Goodson (8)
Woodland View Middle School

Life In Space

Looking into the mysterious world
Magical noises sparkle through the sky
The Milky Way sprinkles into your eyes
Diamonds circle round Saturn,
Uranus, like my head when I bump into my bed
When I look down from above
People and cars look like little ants
The sky up here is red and black
Whizzing rockets whizz by me
See the lumps far away
Bursting like bubbles
I can see a spot so far away
I think it is a planet
Space is brilliant from everywhere
Maybe you could go there!

Hannah Fox (8)
Woodland View Middle School

Space

From Mercury the smallest planet to Jupiter the biggest.
Jupiter, Saturn, Uranus with their rings of gas.
The multicolours representing the parts of the planets.
With the whooshing of the rockets and the whooshing of
                                    the shooting stars.
Asteroids shooting down like balls of fire nearly hitting the planets.
The crashing of the spaceships landing on planets to see if there
                                    is life on them.
The twinkling of the stars shining brightly in the pitch-black sky.
I find it exciting to look at the stars and some make pictures.
Pluto is frozen and Mercury is crisp.

Liam Smith (8)
Woodland View Middle School

Winter Poem

W inter is freezing cold
I ce on the floor
N ights are getting longer
T rees die down
E veryone gets ready for Christmas
R ain and snow is the winter weather

W onderful snowmen when I look outside
O n Christmas Eve everyone gets excited
N ew year is coming
D ead leaves on the floor
E xciting features everywhere
R ivers are frozen over with ice.

Jaydene Guyton (8)
Woodland View Middle School

Space!

When you look up to space
You see lots of stars, planets and a moon,
Venus, Mercury, Earth, Mars, Jupiter, Saturn,
Uranus, Neptune, Pluto.
You see shooting stars,
It's magical, mysterious to be in space.
Space is endless, exciting.
Saturn and Uranus are planets that
Have three gas rings around them.
I would like to be an astronaut because
I would like to float and see all the planets.
It is quiet because I am the only one here.

Abigail Clements (8)
Woodland View Middle School

The Space Poem

I pretend I am an astronaut
Looking down on the planets
Pluto, Mars and Earth, my home
My little tiny home, it looks as small as an ant
My food floating around and I just can't catch it
I look out into space at all the stars
It feels kind of funny
I'm in a zooming space rocket
Twinkling droplets shooting past
I can see Uranus
Saturn has a ring around it
It is just magical to go into space.

Hannah Airdrie (8)
Woodland View Middle School

A Victorian Boy At Work

I like potato picking, I think it's great,
I would do it till half-past eight.
I don't really like picking stones
And my master really moans.
I like collecting eggs,
But it always hurts my legs.

I like the horse he's really kind,
When the blacksmith puts his shoes on he doesn't mind.
The work is hard,
In the yard.
The sheep are as soft as silk,
The cows give us a lot of milk.
The pigs really stink,
Well that's what I think.

The chickens are funny,
I don't get much money,
I like talking to the lady's maid,
If the master catches me I won't get paid.

Peter Broughton (11)
Woodland View Middle School

Bonfire Night

See the pretty colours,
As they sparkle in the sky,
They scream in the wind,
As they shoot up so high.

Hear the bonfire crackle,
See the flames dance in the wind,
Smell the burgers on the barbecue,
Think of Guy Fawkes burning on the bonfire.

See the Catherine wheel spin,
As sparks of colour fly out,
They hypnotise you by spinning,
See the rockets shoot up high.

The fireworks go up so high,
Some of them see spaceships
Some fly to the moon,
But most of them stay in sight.

Kieran Long (8)
Woodland View Middle School

Winter Poem

W rap up warm wear hats, gloves and coats
I n your house put the fire up high so you won't get a chill
  in your middle.
N ice warm bed ready to get in after you have been outside
T here is freezing frost on the freezing cold ground
E veryone slipping and sliding over in the icy puddles
R ivers full of crackling ice

P uddles look like bricks of ice but beware they are slippery
O n winter days you can make snowmen and snow women
E verything is white and foggy
M ountains covered with white snow not one piece of green showing.

Georgie Locke (9)
Woodland View Middle School

Winter

W ind is blowing against us
    We try to stop it
    We get our gloves, hats, coats and boots
    So we can keep warm
I ce and frost freeze us
    We have to keep warm
N ew Year's Eve is soon coming
    Snow is starting to fall, crispy, crunchy
    Snow that freezes you
T iny snowflakes dropping down
    The big, huge snowflakes come down
E venings are getting darker
    We put our reflectors on our coats
    So we don't get run over.
R ain is falling very hard onto the ground
    We keep shelter so we don't get wet
    From the rain and hail

P eople start to celebrate and have
    A lovely Christmas meal.
O ur family and friends start to get excited
    Because it's started to snow.
E veryone loves winter because of the snow and frost.
M ums and dads give us presents.

Tom Johnson (8)
Woodland View Middle School

Bonfire Poem

The fire is crackling.
The guy is burning.
Everybody is wearing gloves and hats.
The rockets are going *bang* in the air.
Going up in the dark black sky.
There's lots of colourful fireworks.
Blue, green, yellow, red and how they flash.
Everybody is watching the fireworks.
Everybody is cheering, the guy is burnt.
It's over then all there was left was ashes.
On the floor and the people had all gone home.

Ricki Guyton (8)
Woodland View Middle School

Bonfire Night

Sizzling hot dogs, screaming rockets, bursting in the sky
Bang! Go the bangers.
Bright spinning Catherine wheels go round and round.
The fire is going, the guy's almost gone.
Bang! Goes a banger.
The dark sky is lit up by reds, greens and blues.
'Wow!' say the children as the last banger bangs.

Jack James (8)
Woodland View Middle School

Love

Love is purple,
It smells like bubble bath,
Love tastes like candyfloss,
It sounds like birds singing,
It feels softer than a baby's bum.
Love lives in *Heaven.*

Jessica Wright-Carruthers (9)
Woodland View Middle School

Volcano Poem

Peaceful and quiet then a shake and then
Exploding lava zoomed out
Rocks and boulders crashed down
People scared and afraid
Lumpy and the bashing noise
As rocks jumping down
Some people need first aid
Killing, melting, screaming hot
Bubbling bubbles, fire and gases
Animals ran fast away
Children crying for help
Ear-splitting earaches
Plants getting crispy
Screaming loudly
It smells of rotten eggs
Eyes watering, choking like hell
Roaring, blasting, the horrible smell
Then the river of fire cools down
Everyone jumps for joy.

Charlie Warren (8)
Woodland View Middle School

Fireworks

F ireworks exploding in the sky
I love watching the colours zoom into the sky
R eaching in the sky trying to touch them
E xplore the fireworks with me and my friends
W arm coats on to keep you warm and safe
O h keep me safe!
R umbling Catherine wheels spinning in the air
K eep away from sparklers with our gloves
S hining in the sky.

Josie Burnham (8)
Woodland View Middle School

Fireworks

Fireworks flashing
Fireworks bright
All you will see is a beautiful sight

In the night
You will see a firework soaring
Straight up into the starry sky

Fireworks going up into
The cold, cold night

Fireworks going, going up
Then go *bang!* And then go *boom!*
Zoom! Go the fireworks

Beautiful colours red, green and brown

The colours are great
Explosives going *boom!*
Catherine wheels *zoom, zoom!* On the gate.

Iain Dix (9)
Woodland View Middle School

Autumn Poem

Autumn is alive
Conkers are falling like rockets of rain
Birds lined up ready to fly south to the sun
Autumn is here bringing gifts from above
It is time for picking apples
We can pick up leaves
Red, yellow, orange
And crackling branches too
People say it is a wonderful day
When autumn flies away.

Elizabeth Fiddy (9)
Woodland View Middle School

Outer Space

Outer space, no gravity, no air
Gigantic asteroids shooting about
Planets, Mars, Jupiter, Venus, Earth, Uranus, Saturn
Mercury, Neptune and Pluto
Boiling hot sun
People in space station in rockets
Dazzling, glimmering, shining stars
Shooting stars flying about
Dark, scary, cold
Black holes sucking things in
The moon orbiting the Earth, does nothing else
Satellites bring us weather and sky
Jupiter massive, the biggest
Pluto the coldest, the smallest
Stars millions and billions
Space probes exploring different planets
Dazzling shooting stars.

Jack Mollicone (9)
Woodland View Middle School

Outer Space

Outer space is a world of its own
We are in outer space, don't moan!
Stars glimmering, shining and swinging
We are in a spacecraft with lots of gadgets and even a phone
Look over there, satellites and a shooting star
If you look far!

There's Mars dancing with shooting stars,
No machines and stuff like motorbikes or cars,
Gloomy and dark, bright comets spinning in orbit,
Stars millions of miles away sucked into black holes.
Pluto cold and shivery and Saturn boiling hot
Space, space, a super place!

Harry Partner (9)
Woodland View Middle School

Love And Hate

Love

Love is violet
It smells like sweet perfume
Love tastes like rich wine
It sounds like doves twittering
It feels like soft velvet
Love lives in your heart.

Hate

Hate is black
It smells like lava
Hate tastes prickly and bitter
It sounds like a boiling kettle
It feels like pins and needles
Hate lives in Hell.

Savannah Foster (9)
Woodland View Middle School

Hope And Unhappiness

Hope

Hope is a light purple,
It smells like tasty strawberries,
Hope tastes like fluffy candyfloss,
It sounds like birds in the morning,
It feels like a water fountain.
Hope lives on a football pitch.

Unhappiness

Unhappiness is a dark grey,
It smells like a man's socks,
Unhappiness tastes like mouldy bread,
It sounds like a noisy chainsaw,
It feels like stinging ulcers,
Unhappiness lives in a smelly dungeon.

Liam Ogle (9)
Woodland View Middle School

Snowfall

S now falls from the sky, settles like a carpet,
N ow it is here, we can build an igloo,
O h how it glistens on the ground,
W hite, wet, cold blizzard, it shimmers in the sun,
 I cicles hang from the rooftops,
N ow let's make a snow angel,
G o get our sledges and have some fun.

Bethany Wade (10)
Woodland View Middle School

Happiness

Happiness is bright yellow,
It smells like vanilla ice cream,
Happiness tastes like a juicy apple,
It sounds like a lively electric guitar,
It feels like a fluffy puppy.
Happiness lives in our hearts.

Luke Plumstead (9)
Woodland View Middle School

Hope

Hope is blue,
It smells like fresh green grass,
Hope tastes like strawberries,
It sounds like a violin,
It feels like butterflies in your tummy.
Hope lives in the church.

Connor Elliott (9)
Woodland View Middle School

Winter Wonderland

S now is glistening like a carpet of glitter
N o! Don't knock my snowman down
O h! Look it's snowing let's go outside
W ow! Dad's made a massive snowman
F lickering as it falls from the blue sky
L oads and loads of it. We could make an igloo
A ngels on the ground in the silky snow
K icking the fresh, pure snow around the garden
E ndless blizzards all around the world.

Charlotte Curson (9)
Woodland View Middle School

Snow

A blanket of snow covers everything,
Footsteps uncover bits of summer,
Snowmen on patrol.
Glistening icicles hang down.

Trees are covered in white,
It's a winter wonderland,
Everyone wrapped up warm.
Watch out for ice.

Pure and sparkly snow everywhere,
The air is fresh and clean,
People having fun.
Winter has just begun.

Shaun Earl (9)
Woodland View Middle School

Snow Day

Snow is shimmering white,
Snow twinkles in the light,
Snow feels like candyfloss,
Snow shines like lipgloss,
Snow is fresh, clean and pure,
This will be your magic cure.

Charlotte Stephens (10)
Woodland View Middle School

Outer Space

'Oh look! There's the sun!
Orbit! Orbit!'
Says the moon
But it's quite fun!

Oh gosh! there's the moon
It's as white as a feather
With little craters!
We will be back soon!

'Get out of my way!'
Says the black hole
'Or you will get sucked up
So go away!'

Oh! It's very cold
We must be near Pluto
Pluto is very . . .
Old!

Oh must we go?
Because . . .
It's brilliant!

Because there's dazzling stars
Oh gosh it's getting hot
We must be near . . .
Mars!

Poppy Segger (8)
Woodland View Middle School

Outer Space

Comets whizz here and there,
Where there is no gravity or air.
Places where people have never been before,
But people who live there might find it a bore.
Spacecrafts like Beagle II,
Could see things that you or I couldn't do.

Rockets zoom to other galaxies in a flash,
But if you don't look where you're going
You could crash!
Some believe in aliens and some do not,
Then they might abduct you and put you in a pot.
Space is a wonderful place where you can't go in cars,
And if I could go to outer space I would go to *Mars!*

Adam Cooper (9)
Woodland View Middle School

Outer Space

Up in space I can see shimmering stars and zooming comets.
I can float like a feather in a spacecraft when there is no gravity.
The sun is boiling and the heat is unbearable.
The sky is so dark and black but not empty
Because galaxies, stars and planets are stored in this place.

There are probes and rockets blasting out into space,
Exploring the universe, Neptune, Venus, Mercury, Mars,
Jupiter, Saturn and Uranus,
All these planets waiting to be explored.
Is there life out there?
I don't know, but I love space, it's cosmic!

Matthew Rolls (9)
Woodland View Middle School

Bonfire Poem

F amilies joining together to see the flying, fabulous fireworks,
I love the colours.
R ed, green, yellow and all of the colours you could think of,
E choes through the night and the fireworks are so good.
W onderful, flashing, flying fireworks.
O thers joining together to see the fireworks.
R ings of people have fun as the fireworks go off,
K ids smiling, holding pretty sparklers.
S ausages and burgers sizzling on a barbecue.

Georgina Fiddy (9)
Woodland View Middle School

Autumn

Rubies fall swiftly to the ground.
Heat going up and dew coming down.
Conkers hatching from husks.
Leaves are turning red swirling up and down.
Squirrels searching for nuts in the crispy, crunchy leaves.

The autumn winds whistling round and round,
Birds fly south, winds blow north.
How many leaves will live out this year?
From smooth sparkling green to rough, crispy brown.

Combine harvesters moving up and down.
Gleaming rain bouncing off of spiders' webs.
Hedgehog, rabbit, bear and mouse, hibernating everywhere.

The autumn rains blowing north,
When will it be autumn?
I hope it's time to go conkering,
Hazelnuts falling,
Crispy leaves are falling,
Gleaming rain is falling,

Hooray . . . it's autumn!

Luke Forder (8)
Woodland View Middle School

Bonfire Poem

F ireworks explode in the dark sky
I nteresting colours up high say goodbye
R ockets going higher
E veryone eating hot dogs
W ow! Everyone says
O utstanding bangs
R ain has gone, darkness has come
K eep back, don't get hurt
S ounds of them make some of us jump!

Sabrina Ives (9)
Woodland View Middle School

All About Space

Mercury is the smallest planet.
Jupiter is the biggest planet and it has a faint red ring around it.
Saturn and Uranus have one too.
Milky Way is a bunch of stars.
It is quiet and dusty.
You cannot see the sun.
Big, bright, sparkly stars.
Space is endless.
Astronauts are excited to go up.
It is magical in space.
If it is your first time there it could be mysterious.
Mercury is the closest planet to the sun.
The sun is a big fireball.

Laura Bezants (9)
Woodland View Middle School

Winter Poem

W e will shiver all through the winter
  I n the warm and cosy house trying to get out of the cold
N ow we can make snowmen
T he cars are covered in ice and frost
E ars are getting colder and colder
R eading a new book in front of the fire

P eople are getting cold
O ur voices look like smoke
E veryone is going ice skating
M ums wrap you up in warm clothes.

Sam Dootson (8)
Woodland View Middle School

The Sparkly Night

F lashing colours in the sky
  I like fireworks rushing high
R ed, yellow, green, silver and gold
E normous bangs in the night
W hizzing Catherine wheels
O range fireworks above my head
R ockets zooming
K ids around the bonfire
S parklers glowing in the night.

Kelly Kemp (8)
Woodland View Middle School

Snowy Days

W et snow melts to water
 I mpeccable ice makes you slip and slide
N ew year seems so far away
T inkly icicles flash to the ground
E very piece of snow falls from the sky
R eally snow is water.

W et rain turns to ice
O verwhelmed, feel happy
N early built a snowman
D ripping snow hits your nose
E very animal goes to sleep
R ight in front of you is a snowball.

Jamie North (8)
Woodland View Middle School

Autumn

There are leaves crunching and crackling like a bonfire,
The wind is howling,
There are conkers falling quickly out of the trees,
Birds are flying south as fast as a train,
I think autumn is magic.

I hear birds tweeting,
I can smell fresh grass being cut and smoky air.
I feel the cobwebs fly in my face.
Brown, golden, red, orange, yellow leaves
Falling like racing paper.
The clouds are milky blue and white.
This is the start of autumn.

Matthew Leggett (8)
Woodland View Middle School

Winter

W e go outside to have a snowball fight
　　but then we want to build a snowman to show Mum,
　　she will be impressed.
'I cy' we say as we slip along the path
　　oh no we have fallen over we try to get up but we can't!
N ippy and cold we say to each other, 'Our fingers and toes
　　are numb,' we say
T rees have no leaves but when it snows it has white leaves
　　they sparkle and look silver
E veryone let's have a celebration because it is nearly Christmas
R eindeer are coming I am so excited

P ut your hat on and your scarf and your gloves and your coat on too
O ur family is excited because it's nearly Christmas
'E veryone it is winter!' shouts a little boy
M um shouts to everyone to tell them it is tea.

Bethany Golden (9)
Woodland View Middle School

Winter Poem

Winter is coming soon
Icicles hanging from windows
Nothing as good as a snowball fight
Time to put all your warm clothes on
Everyone is sliding on ice
Red hands and noses are freezing cold
Plants are dying as soon as winter is here
Only snow always makes you build snowmen
Every day we have to defrost the car

Jamie Chamberlin (8)
Woodland View Middle School

Death

Death is dark black,
It smells like a sewer,
Death tastes like mouldy chocolate,
It sounds like a rock band that can't play,
It feels like a sharp pain,
Death lives in a graveyard.

Chloe Sarsby (10)
Woodland View Middle School

An Autumn Poem

Autumn is great
The leaves change colour
Red, yellow, orange and brown
What a beautiful sight
The nights are getting darker
It gets windy every day
The days are getting shorter
My birthday is very soon
I can't wait!
The smell of the air is beautiful
The leaves are rustling like a baby's rattle
Winter is very near
The leaves are falling, dancing off the trees
That makes a carpet of leaves
They are crunching and breaking
The wind is very strong
It is getting very cold
Birds migrate
Animals hibernate
Conkers fall off, people play conker fights
I'm in Year 4 now, I'm getting older.

Micaela Robinson (9)
Woodland View Middle School